Perfect Phrases for
College Application Essays

Also available from McGraw-Hill

Perfect Phrases for Performance Reviews by Douglas Max and Robert Bacal

Perfect Phrases for Performance Goals by Douglas Max and Robert Bacal

Perfect Solutions for Difficult Employee Situations by Sid Kemp

Perfect Phrases for Customer Service by Robert Bacal

Perfect Phrases for Business Proposals and Business Plans by Don Debelak

Perfect Phrases for Executive Presentations by Alan Perlman

Perfect Phrases for the Sales Call by William Brooks

Perfect Phrases for Lead Generation by William Brooks

Perfect Phrases for Sales and Marketing Copy by Barry Callen

Perfect Phrases for Writing Grant Proposals by Dr. Beverly Browning

Perfect Phrases for College Application Essays

Hundreds of Ready-to-Use Phrases to Write a Compelling Essay and Catch the Attention of an Admissions Committee

Sheila Bender

McGraw-Hill

New York   Chicago   San Francisco   Lisbon
London   Madrid   Mexico City   Milan   New Delhi
San Juan   Seoul   Singapore   Sydney   Toronto

1 2 3 4 5 6 7 8 9 0 DOC/DOC 0 1 2 3 1 0 9 8

ISBN 978-0-07-154603-4
MHID 0-07-154603-0

This is a *CWL Publishing Enterprises Book* produced for McGraw-Hill by CWL Publishing Enterprises, Inc., Madison, Wisconsin, www.cwlpub.com.

This publication is designed to provide accurate and authoritative information in regard to the subject matter covered. It is sold with the understanding that neither the author nor the publisher is engaged in rendering legal, accounting, or other professional services. If legal advice or other expert assistance is required, the services of a competent professional person should be sought.

> —From a Declaration of Principles jointly adopted by a Committee
> of the American Bar Association and a Committee of Publishers

McGraw-Hill books are available at special quantity discounts to use as premiums and sales promotions, or for use in corporate training programs. To contact a representative, please visit the Contact Us pages at www.mhprofessional.com.

For Linda Abraham, president of Accepted.com, for her many years of mentoring me as I worked with her college and graduate school applicant clients.

To my children Emily and Seth Bender, whose college essays were remarkable and for my grandsons, Toby and Rafe Menon. May this book serve you well when it is time.

Contents

Contents

Contents

Contents

Contents

Contents

Preface

The Meaning of Perfect Phrases

I have been helping high school students with the process of writing their college application essays for over two decades as a professional writer, as a mother of my own two college-bound kids, as a community college and university instructor helping those transferring to other schools, and as an editor for admissions consulting company Accepted.com.

In my work, I help students interview themselves to find the material that will make a good essay and help them shape their experiences into lively, rich prose.

With *Perfect Phrases for College Application Essays*, my goal is to lead students on the page, as I have in person, on the adventure of inventing, drafting, and polishing application essays that exude integrity, cohesion, authenticity, self-reflection, thought, and analysis.

When I was asked to write for the Perfect Phrases series, I realized that the title's phrase "perfect phrases" is meant to be inspiring, an invitation, and a warm welcome to entering a process. For me, perfect phrases expresses my pleasure at being able to lend you a hand. It makes me think of ordering in a restaurant, when the server asks for my order and then cheerfully says, "Perfect." They approve of my choice, and they will be instrumental in making sure I get what I asked for.

Perfect phrases will help you make choices and order the "meal" you want. The "perfect phrases" in the title does not mean you have to use the phrases included here exactly as they're given. Rather, these are meant to stimulate and inspire and provide examples of what works that you can modify and make your own.

Essays that work sound like you, show something about you that readers cannot otherwise find out from the application materials, and catch the admissions committee members' interest and maintain it. In this book, my goal is to help you feel secure that your writing tells your story and evokes your individual perceptions.

In her book, *How to Write a Killer College Application*, Katherine Cohen writes, "a few things remain clear about the college essay:

1. It must reflect your personality and your voice.
2. It must shed light on significant aspects of your character and experience, providing insight into you both as a scholar and a human being.
3. It should be an intimate and lively portrait of yourself that none of the other applicants can provide.
4. If the application in question asks you to comment on a work of literature or art, you must still relate the cultural object in question back to yourself and your personal experience.
5. I you are asked why you are applying to a particular school, you should discuss how the school's offerings relate to your personal interests.

6. No matter what the topic, all essays essentially ask the same
   question: **What makes you tick?**"

Cohen puts those last words in bold because the purpose of
college application essays is to make readers feel they are meeting you, enjoying your company, and getting to know you. The
only way this can happen is if there is real experience on the
page, not summaries or mere recitations of what already appears
in the application materials.

This can't happen if the writer doesn't take the time to hang
out with the essay's readers and really show them something.
This can't happen if the writer uses generic experience. And this
can't happen if the candidate's application raises questions that
the essays don't address.

For example, if you had oddly low grades one year or didn't
do well on the SAT or had to make up classes in summer school,
the essay is your chance to explain what's going on. If there is
something in the transcripts and application that will raise a red
flag for the admissions committee, choose an essay topic that
allows you to explain yourself. It may be hard to turn things
around by writing about what was going on, but this builds inti-
macy and allows readers to feel that they are in touch with the
real you. Explaining the reasons behind dips in grades or drop-
ping out of school or clubs or extracurricular activities also allows
you, the writer, to see more clearly the pressures you were dealing with and what you learned through the experience.

In the film *City of Angels*, Nicolas Cage's character, an immortal
from the spiritual plain who lacks the human's five senses, asks the
mortal he is in love with, Meg Ryan's character, what a pear tastes
like. She says something like, "You know; it tastes like a pear." He
replies, "But what does a pear taste like to you?"

Preface

That's the trick—to write what your experience tastes like, sounds like, smells like, looks like, and feels like to you—whether you're writing about a work of art, literature, a social problem, someone who influenced you, being on an athletic team, winning an award, doing community service, or surviving hardship. The readers of your essay want to enter the world through your senses. In doing so, they connect with you, understanding what you value and why, how you think, and what you create from your opportunities.

The perfect phrases in this book, along with an understanding of the steps that help you answer specific essay application questions, will help you effectively communicate who you are and what you believe. Your essay will introduce you to admissions committee readers. These are people who want to get to know you and how you'll contribute to making the incoming freshman class the best ever.

Each of the phrases in this book is meant to help you research and present yourself in an organized and intriguing manner. Reading and working with the phrases will guide your writing from the spark of inspiration through the development of a compelling beginning, middle, and end. They will help make the process of writing essays for your applications less painful and more rewarding than it might otherwise seem.

Acknowledgments

With thanks to the hundreds of students with whom I have worked over 20-plus years to find the compelling parts of their life experience. Your situations and solutions are forever with me. I have drawn from and embellished them to write composites as samples for shaping college application essays.

About the Author

Sheila Bender publishes *Writing It Real* at **www.writingitreal.com**. She began her career as a junior high school English teacher with a Masters of Arts in Teaching. After receiving a Master's degree in Creative Writing, she began teaching freshman composition at colleges and universities. She has worked for Accepted.com, a company that coaches and tutors candidates in writing essays for their college and graduate school applications.

Sheila published her first book about writing, *Writing in a Convertible with the Top Down*, in 1991 and has continued since then writing and publishing poetry (*Sustenance: New and Selected Poems*), reviews (in *Poet Lore*, *The Seattle Times* and *The World*), and articles (*Writer's Digest* and *The Writer*), as well as producing and publishing seven more books on writing (most recently, *Writing and Publishing Personal Essays*). Others include: *Writing Personal Essays*, *Writing Personal Poetry*, *A Year in the Life*, and *Keeping a Journal You Love*.

In the last 15 years, Sheila has provided teacher training in Washington, Arizona, and California. In 2002, she conceived and launched *Writing It Real* at **www.writingitreal.com** as a vehicle to help others foster their best work, involve themselves in a community of people who write from personal experience, and learn to teach others how to facilitate good writing.

She has an undergraduate degree in English from the University of Wisconsin, an MAT in secondary education from Keane College in New Jersey, and an MA in creative writing from the University of Washington.

Part One

Building a Foundation for Writing Your Essay

Part One

Building a Conversational
Program

Chapter 1
Writing the College Application Essay Is a Daunting Task: What to Do About It

Writing the college application essay is a daunting task because, as the writer, your mission is to present yourself on paper as the interesting, reflective, and exciting person you truly are. Although you have most likely done this many times in person among friends and with teachers and group leaders, doing it through writing involves overcoming hurdles you might not experience in personal contact with people. During personal interaction, you have the other people's questions to help you include information and best explain what you mean. You can also read their expressions and know how they feel about what you're telling them. That way you figure out where to add more and where to focus your conversation.

Most often, when you talk you don't have to work at sounding like yourself. But when you're writing the college application essay, the formality of the task can lead you to adopt a tone or phrasing that sounds like you're trying too hard. On the other hand, shying away from what seems like too much formality, you might inadvertently adopt a tone that is so colloquial or humble that your writing draws only a faint or blurry picture of who you are. It's also possible that you might take the details of your experience for granted and leave out important ones, keeping your essay from helping you stand out in the minds of the admissions committee.

Stanford University advises applicants to have their parents and friends read their application essays to help ensure that the tone is right. And then there is this advice:

> In reading your writing, we want to hear your individual voice. Write essays that reflect who you are; use specific, concrete details and write in a natural style. Begin work on these essays early, and feel free to ask your parents, teachers, and friends to provide constructive feedback. When you ask for feedback on an essay draft, ask if the essay's tone sounds like your voice. It should. Your parents, teachers, and friends know you better than anyone. If they don't believe that your essay captures who you are, how you write, or what you believe, surely the admissions committee will be unable to recognize what's most distinctive about you.

If you're among (1) those who think their most important story is too personal to share with adults they don't know, (2) those who don't like to focus attention on themselves, (3) those who have a difficult time recognizing what distinguishes them from others, or (4) those who don't believe their writing skills are strong enough to do a good job of putting experience on the page, you may have difficulty starting and finishing an effective college application essay. To get the job done well you'll have to become comfortable using details and examples from your experience to back up your assertions about personal attributes, lessons learned, goals, and interests in college.

Trusting in the significance of your life experiences and writing honestly about them are what make an essay compelling to admissions committee members. You need them to recall your essay from among thousands. Luckily, there are perfect phrases and techniques that can help you overcome writing difficulties. To begin, you must trust that your experiences to date are worth writing about. You also have to realize that counselors really do read personal statements.

In his article "Getting In: the Not-so-Secret Admissions Process," in the Fall 2007 issue of *On Wisconsin*, a magazine for alumni and friends of the University of Wisconsin-Madison campus, Michael Penn writes, "Sure, a Hemingwayesque personal statement won't make up for major deficiencies in other parts of your application, but it's curious that so many students squander a golden opportunity to market themselves. Especially in cases where students have holes in their applications that might leave a counselor wondering—such as a dip in grades due to an illness—a personal statement is a chance to say, 'let me explain …'"

Penn quotes admissions counselor St. Arnauld, "We really rely on that personal statement to get a better sense of where the applicant is coming from and where he or she is going."

Make It a Goal to Trust Your Experience

If you overcome a tendency toward the general when you write assertions about yourself and your experiences, you'll begin writing deeply enough to find fresh insight from the words you put on the page. Show; don't tell. By trusting images (what you saw, heard, tasted, touched, smelled, felt) and details (facts, statistics, the words of those you've read and listened to), you can build a structure that makes you feel comfortable writing about your experiences, thoughts, and perceptions. This will lead to the acknowledgment of important lessons you've learned that will serve as a foundation for adjusting to college, choosing studies, joining clubs and activities, and enhancing the experience of your classmates. There are "perfect phrases" to help you find these connections.

If you approach your writing by believing it will teach you more about yourself than you knew before you wrote the essay (the root meaning of the word *essay* is "to assay," or test), you'll grow as an individual. Your writing will reflect that and show the admissions committee that you're preparing yourself for college by assessing your experience. The poet Robert Frost is often misquoted as saying, "No discovery for the writer, no discovery for the reader." He actually said, "No tears in the writer, no tears in the reader." Either way, Frost was emphasizing that writing is a dynamic process for the writer because the writer is making an inquiry into a chosen subject. When this inquiry through writing is done well, the reader feels how the writer felt discovering an insight or a new meaning. *Feeling* the discovery is part of what makes a memorable essay.

Finding a new way to organize your experience using the perfect phrases I offer, you'll discover new meaning in your experience, whether that experience seems very ordinary or extraordinary. You'll be able to use your essay to show others what you have come to see in yourself.

Writing the College Application Essay Is a Daunting Task

As Sarah Myers McGinty (author of *The College Application Essay*) writes:

> In this case, you look into your life, select an element, event, experience, or insight, and assign a meaning to it: that fateful summer, that wonderful biology class, that meaningful job at the ice cream parlor, that exciting lunch I might have had with Charles Darwin. Then you prove the validity of that meaning, backing up and substantiating the view you have taken.

Let the perfect phrases in this book help you travel this route to discovery as you offer details from your experience, your reading, your activities, and your reflections. While examining the variety of essay questions on college applications, I'll show you how to use these phrases to enhance your writing.

Chapter 2
A Look at the Application
Essay Questions

For the 2007–2008 academic year, total membership in the Common Application, Inc. has risen to 315 schools, including 18 public institutions. The addition of schools from South Dakota and Utah means that 43 states plus the District of Columbia and Qatar are represented by schools accepting the Common Application. The application requires one essay of 250 words minimum and one supplemental essay of 150 words maximum. The longer essay must be on one of six topics. Until recently there was a limit of 500 words on the longer essay, but fall 2007 and spring 2008 applicants currently have no word limit on the longer essay.

In its history statement, the Common Application, Inc. says:

The Common Application membership association was established in 1975 by 15 private colleges that wished to provide a common, standardized first-year application form for use at any member institution. With the administrative support of the National Association of Secondary School Principals

(NASSP), the organization grew steadily throughout its first 30 years.

Now in our fourth decade, the Common Application currently provides both online and print versions of its First-year and Transfer Applications. Our membership of more than 300 institutions now represents the full range of higher education institutions in the US: public and private, large and small, highly selective and modestly selective, and East Coast, West Coast, and every region in between.

To see if the schools you're applying to use The Common Application, visit: http://app.commonapp.org.

The question selection for 2007–2008 includes:

1. Evaluate a significant experience, achievement, risk you have taken, or ethical dilemma you have faced and its impact on you.
2. Discuss some issue of personal, local, national, or international concern and its importance to you.
3. Indicate a person who has had a significant influence on you, and describe that influence.
4. Describe a character in fiction, a historical figure, or a creative work (as in art, music, science, etc.) that has had an influence on you, and explain that influence.
5. A range of academic interests, personal perspectives, and life experiences adds much to the educational mix. Given your personal background, describe an experience that illustrates what you would bring to the diversity in a college community, or an encounter that demonstrated the importance of diversity to you.
6. Topic of your choice.

Even though you can get away with the shorter 250-word essay, shorter essays are often harder to write than longer ones, and using the allotted space completely will allow you to more fully evoke your experiences through examples and details. However, be careful that a longer essay (500–700 words is ideal) doesn't wander.

In addition to an essay written in answer to one of these questions, the Common Application requires you to write one short answer of 150 words or fewer about one of your activities. The question for the short answer is phrased this way: "Please briefly elaborate on one of your activities (extracurricular, personal activities, or work experience)."

Most school-specific questions are versions of those on the Common Application. I'll show you how to create answers for the Common Application questions that will work for schools that don't use the Common Application. In this way, you may be able to apply a Common Application essay to other applications as well. Conversely, shaping answers for school-specific supplemental and non-Common Application questions can help you add dimension to what you write for the Common Application question you choose. I'll examine some school-specific questions and explain how to work with them.

A good strategy to adopt is this one: If any of the schools you're applying to use the Common Application, before you decide which Common Application question you're going to answer, look at the questions on all the applications of the schools you're applying to. This will make you aware of non–Common Application main essays and supplemental long- and short-answer questions. You want to be sure you can use a version of the main essay you write for many schools, and you want to be sure you use all the questions a school asks you to answer to create a complete package that shows off as much about you, your experiences, thinking, and skills as possible. You'll see that most questions are versions of the Common Application questions, and they all provide opportunities for you to reveal how you think, what your values and goals are, and what you've experienced in the world, whether that has been through travel, activities, family and community life, or studies. Therefore, learning strategies for how to answer the six Common Application questions will help you with all your application essays.

Some of the Common Application questions, such as numbers 2 and 4, offer particular help for those who don't like to talk about themselves by moving the focus to something outside of themselves.

Question 5 is valuable for students who come from immigrant families or ethnic minorities because it allows students to discuss values and experiences as well as obstacles they've successfully overcome. The question also works for nonminority students with significant experience that has prepared them for appreciating diversity in college. A student who founded an International Club in high school might describe the work of establishing the club, the value it held for the school and students, and what everyone—especially he—learned. Someone who participated in an international gymnastics competition may have learned about diversity competing in another country.

There are many ways to discuss diversity: A person who immigrated from Mexico might want to use the experience she had to answer question 2 and discuss the issue of Spanish becoming a national language or the issue of driver's license instructional books being presented in many languages.

To demonstrate how school-specific questions are often really no different from those on the Common Application, let's look at Stanford's two 2006 questions:

"A picture is worth a thousand words" as the adage goes. Sometimes a photo or picture can capture an object that you treasure, a person you admire or a place that you love; sometimes a photograph is simply your record of an experience or moment in your life. Imagine one photo or picture that you have, or would like to have, and tell us why it is meaningful to you.

As you reflect on your life thus far, what has someone said, written, or expressed in some fashion that is especially meaningful to you? Why?

You can see that the first 2006 Stanford question was a way into thinking about an experience or person who influenced you. It also provided a way into discussion of national or local events and situations and your response to them if you, say, chose a picture from the newspaper or a history book or from a family album from historic times or civic events.

The second question allowed applicants to think along the lines of Common Application questions 2, 4, and 5. But a candidate could have also written a diversity essay from this question or the first: If you are a minority or specialize in a particular field such as gymnastics or have an immigrant experience, you might have thought about anything you've heard or been told that carried meaning for you as a member of your group.

The influence question and the photograph question offer the opportunity to show more about your ethnic experience, special talents and commitments, or interest in history and political events. Each question supplies a particular strategy toward insight and requires that the candidate rely on different phrases to create the essay's structure and capture experience for readers.

A Look at the Application Essay Questions

Stanford is now accepting the Common Application, but this process of converting questions will work for schools that aren't Common Application institutions. For instance, the University of Washington wants a personal statement that addresses one of the following: "a character-defining moment, the cultural awareness you've developed, a challenge faced, a personal hardship or barrier overcome."

For a second essay, applicants must choose between "Discuss how your family's experience or cultural history enriched you or presented opportunities or challenges in pursuing your educational goals" and "Tell us a story from your life, describing an experience that either demonstrates your character or helped shaped it." I'm sure you recognize the similarities in these choices to Common Application questions 1, 3, and 5. You might even see a way to shape an answer for Common Application question 2 that would help you address the UW questions: something of local or national concern that you were involved in that would show your character.

Even when a school doesn't use the Common Application, its admissions committee may allow the use of the essay. For instance, the University of Virginia's 2007 application asks for the essay questions to be in two parts of 250 words each. There are different questions for part one depending on which school you are applying to inside the university. There are then six choices for part two. However, an alternative choice is to send an essay you've written for a different school, up to 500 words!

The application says, "If an essay question for another college piqued your interest, feel free to submit your response to that question. Please limit your submission to one page, or approximately 500 words."

Help Getting from "Having to Write the Essay" to "Having Written It"

Whatever schools you apply to, when you read through the questions, you'll begin to know which make you most willing to write an essay, even if you don't know how you'll write it. Remember Robert Frost's words that if you're not interested in the exploration, your readers won't be interested either. Moreover, you'll have read the college's Web sites and mission statements and have in mind what they say they're looking for in applicants.

Sarah Lawrence College, for instance, says that it's interested in students who have a diversity of educational goals and are passionate learners:

> As different as their interests and pursuits are from each other, our students share a few essential characteristics: they are inquisitive, they are adventurous, and they are passionate learners. They seek connections between the arts and the sciences, between the historical and the contemporary. They are as comfortable confronting primary texts as they are confident pursuing lines of original thought.
>
> Additionally, a student's contributions to their community and time spent outside the classroom through extracurricular activities will be considered.

An applicant serious about entering Sarah Lawrence would have this in mind when choosing a question. No matter what the material in the answer, it will need to be presented in ways that demonstrate the student's commitment to learning and to making connections across the curriculum. If an applicant to Sarah Lawrence feels that community service doesn't jump off the page of her application, she might want to write about one community service effort, no matter how small, that taught her an important lesson and helped her link it to her thinking and experience.

A Look at the Application Essay Questions

No writer knows ahead of time exactly what he or she is going to say on the page. However, it is important to think about how to pair your experience and interests with particular questions to demonstrate that you are exactly the kind of applicant the school says it's looking for.

Your ideas might be in the back of your mind as you write, but one sentence will lead to another and to paragraphs and to pages, and you will bring what has been unarticulated to the page. After your words are on the page, look at them and seek to discern a shape to your experience. Use that to organize the flow of your essay in a way that informs, garners insight, and shows the readers you are the incarnation of the applicant they have described in broad strokes. This is where the interest lies for you as a writer and for your readers. The perfect phrases in the next part of the book will help you mine yourself for experiences to use in answering the application questions.

As you use the perfect phrases in the following chapters to answer specific questions, you'll gain assistance in staying on course for finding your story, its details, assertions, and meaning. You'll find the shape that makes the essay and its story compelling. And these phrases will help you find ways to organize your essay so readers can easily follow it.

When you're done writing, you'll have learned more than you ever thought you could from shaping the events of your life for the page. The reader will be impressed at the journey you've taken. Creating an essay is, after all, the opportunity to use the craft of writing to find out what you've been thinking and take your thinking to the next level.

Now, on to the perfect phrases that will help you gather your thoughts and experiences for writing the essays.

Part Two

Perfect Phrases for Developing and Writing College Application Essays

Chapter 3
Perfect Phrases for Inventorying Experiences That Highlight Your Attributes and Attitudes

There are many roads into finding material for essays that show what you will bring to universities that accept you. Some of these roads help you show what you have learned through achievements and education, and others help you explain personal attributes and attitudes.

I like what Sarah Myers McGinty writes in *The College Application Essay*: "What you want to show is your intensity, enthusiasm, insight, and understanding. It is, after all, what the college wants to see. It's what they hope to measure in the essay and what you'll need to succeed when you're accepted." She writes that the college you're applying to "has questions about you partly because you still have questions about yourself. But the essay is a chance to demonstrate which questions you've asked yourself and what answers you've found."

In other words, finding a road into writing a vivid essay is a way of testing, doing the *assay* (from which the word essay derives) to show who you are. The essay shows admissions committee readers the applicant's priorities, values, and ability to synthesize information and to learn through experience. It also highlights his or her creative mind and depth of understanding concerning life's intellectual and social issues.

The hardest part of writing the essay that will put you in a wonderful light is finding the springboard experience from which to jump into the waters of your inquiry. So before you begin to develop your essays, take some time to reflect on the answers to as many of the following perfect phrases questions as you can. They will help you focus on yourself—which is the start of writing your college application essay.

The answers you write will inform you about interesting aspects of yourself that are suitable for answering the application essay questions. Using these perfect phrases for inventorying yourself will also help you prepare for college interviews, write short answers about your activities, and create addendums required to discuss lower-than-desired grades and test scores or gaps in your schooling.

Perfect Phrases for Focusing on Significant Personal Achievement

Have you won awards that you're proud of?

- I am pleased to have been chosen as board representative for my school and plan to bring my classmates' concerns to the attention of the adults who run our district school board.
- I am a member of my school's honor society and am proud of my achievement because it reminds me of how hard I have worked to achieve my goal of preparing well for college.
- I have played on my school's football team since I was a sophomore. Last year when we made it to the championship, I scored the winning touchdown. I'm proud to have scored, but I know I was not alone. The whole team contributed to our win.

Have you contributed to a person or group in a way that makes you proud?

- As student council president, I'm proud that I initiated a program that enrolled senior citizens in a special lecture series at our school so students can benefit from the knowledge base in our community.
- I am proud to have organized a club called Small Business Entrepreneurs at my school. This gave me a chance to meet classmates who were also interested in learning business principles, and we helped each other start enterprises to help pay for our college studies.

If you have mastery in playing an instrument or a sport or in understanding a subject, how do you evaluate your mastery?

- Sitting first chair viola in our state high school orchestra, I am proud of my accomplishment but understand how much further I can go with more study and practice.
- I am starting quarterback for my school's football team, and several schools are recruiting me to play on their teams. I know that as well as I play now, I will meet stronger and stronger opponents.
- I am considered the town expert on water creatures in our environs, and I volunteer as a docent at our local marine science center. I look forward to extending my knowledge to other areas of marine biology.

If you have overcome an obstacle, including handicaps, how did doing so help you develop your character and abilities?

- Attending high school in a wheelchair presented many obstacles to overcome personally and socially, but having overcome them, I have gained a stronger commitment to continue my education.
- Entering high school after only two years of studying ESL, I knew I had a long way to go before I could communicate effectively with students and teachers. I used my math skills to help classmates and made many friends, who in turn helped me.
- I have worked 20 to 30 hours a week all through high school. Although the workload has cut into my time for sports and other extracurricular activities, I have learned to manage time well, have earned good grades in my classes, and have made time for community service through my

church where I tutor children in families who have recently arrived in the United States.

If you speak more than one language, how did you learn the language or languages that aren't your native language?

- I speak Russian in addition to English as my parents and grandparents, who live with us, speak together in their native tongue.
- My parents have sent me to after-school Chinese community classes since I was in grade school, and today I am fluent in the language of my parents' country of origin.
- I spent a year abroad in Italy my junior year, and although I didn't know Italian before I went, I came home fairly fluent.

If you immigrated and had to adapt to a new culture, what was the most difficult part of doing that, and how did you succeed?

- Feeling comfortable in western-style clothing was one of the first adaptations I made after arriving in Kansas City from Iran. My parents were all for me doing this, but I was not used to showing my hair in public. I developed a three-step program for myself to get comfortable. That program worked for the next series of difficult adaptations I had to make.
- I want to be a doctor, but my parents believe girls must get married and have children and do not need an extensive education. To convince my parents to allow me to go to college and start on my way to becoming a doctor, I shared information about the numbers of sick people from our ethnic group who do not get appropriate medical attention in their new country.

- Because my parents are much stricter than my friends' parents, I was going to miss out on many social activities and, perhaps, not be able to keep my friendships going. I asked my parents if I could invite friends over for dinner one night a week so we could eat and do homework together. I hoped that once they met my friends from school, they would allow me to join a school club.

Was there a difficult decision you had to make? How did you make it, and what did you learn about yourself in doing so?

- I learned that a friend was involved with drugs. I decided to tell my parents, hoping they would take over by talking to my friend's parents. When they seemed at a loss about what to do because they didn't know the parents, I realized I would have to gain confidence and trust myself.

- When my father got sick, my mother hired a babysitter to stay with my little sister every day after school so I could continue on the cheerleading squad. But I decided to give up the squad and learned that helping my sister when I was sad about our father's illness was as valuable for me as it was for her.

- After doing a required 30 hours of community service for a class last year, I decided to continue working at the Center for Developmentally Disabled Adults. The decision was hard because my responsibilities would increase, and I didn't know if I would be able to work with the adults beyond helping set the table for their snacks as I had been doing. I learned that jumping into a useful activity even when I am afraid helps me see new qualities in myself.

Perfect Phrases for Focusing on Your Interests and How They Shape You

If you are a musician, how does this influence the way you understand the world?

- As a musician, I think a lot about rhythm and harmony and try to apply these principles to understanding others and the world around me.
- Because I perform for groups, I think a lot about making people comfortable and prepared to listen.
- Studying with skilled musicians, I have learned great respect not only for them as teachers but also for those who were their teachers.

If you are a visual artist, how does this influence the way you understand the world?

- As a cartoonist, I am always reading facial expressions and believe that often the unsaid is the strongest communication we have.
- As a painter, I am interested in nature's patterns and mixture of colors. My success in observing and rendering them every season has helped me in chemistry, biology, and physics.
- I enjoy working in mixed media, and creating combinations of foil, beads, paper, felt, and paint has helped me understand the importance of contrasts, whether that be in art, style, or people's opinions.

If you are a writer, how does this influence the way you understand the world?

- Because I keep a journal every day and record what I have heard, seen, touched, tasted, and smelled, I have learned how much information we take in every day through our senses.
- As a member of a writing group, I have been lucky to make the kind of friendships where I can share what is most important to me.
- I write for my school newspaper. In interviewing people, I have learned how important school clubs are for helping people learn.

If you love literature or social science or physical education or law, how does this influence the way you understand the world?

- I love to read and have applied the insights of many famous characters to difficult situations in my life.
- I love studying government and believe that healthy debate, along with clear policy and legal structure, is integral to a strong society.
- I know it might not sound impressive to say my favorite subject is gym. However, learning how to use my body in soccer, yoga, dance, and basketball has helped me understand the importance of the mind-body connection in achieving excellence in all aspects of my life.

If you love helping children or the elderly, how does this influence the way you understand the world?

- I volunteer at a community center for senior citizens, and the amount of experience and wisdom I have acquired there makes me feel more secure about the world.

- I babysit 10 hours a week for a four-year-old and his two-year-old sister. I now know how important it is to learn by doing. In my career as a special education teacher, I hope to help students of all ages with hands-on learning.
- I am a camp counselor each summer, and being around kids learning new skills has helped me remember how continuing to grow and learn leads to productivity.

If the teachings and activities of your church, synagogue, or mosque have affected your interests and activities, what are the results of your experiences?

- My religious training has taught me the value of the Golden Rule.
- My religious training has taught me the value of pausing in my daily rush to reflect on the larger picture.
- My religious training has taught me the value of knowledge handed down from one generation to the next.

Perfect Phrases for Focusing on Character Traits

Are there particular people you admire? How do you know you are developing the traits you most admire in them?

- I used some of the tactics I'd read Gandhi used and adapted them when, as a student council member, I inaugurated a peer review system for addressing misdeeds by students.
- Like Martin Luther King, whose speeches I admire, I have addressed my classmates in assembly on the issue of racism at school.
- My grandfather suffers from a progressive eye disease that is causing him to lose his eyesight; yet his gratitude for life is infectious. Under his influence, I wake up each morning and say thank you for many blessings—interesting classes to attend, food in the refrigerator, a peaceful community to live in.

How has being an athlete influenced your character?

- Because I am an athlete, I have learned perseverance.
- Because I am an athlete, I have learned how to work well on teams.
- Because I am an athlete, I have learned how to mentor others and contribute beyond my personal performance.

How has your deep interest in a particular subject affected you?

- My interest in botany led me to join a 4-H club where I created a composting project adopted by my town.

- My interest in traveling to Turkey one day led me to an internship with a local travel agent. There I learned about running a business and now plan to be a tour guide to ancient cities of the world.
- My passion for ballet led me to join my high school's dance troupe. This year I will dance the lead role in our winter performance, as well as lead a dance program in a local elementary school.

If you have a demanding health or physical or emotional situation, describe what you learned from that experience from having dealt with it.

- I was diagnosed with ADHD when I was in fifth grade. Learning coping skills and a respect for medications has made me an organized and knowledgeable person.
- When my parents divorced and fought for months over custody of my sisters and me, I learned how to draw boundaries so I could focus on my studies and future.
- Because I was diagnosed with childhood diabetes, I have had to learn how to stand up for what is healthy for me and not give in to peer pressure.

How has involvement in a community service program at home or abroad changed you?

- Raising money for Hurricane Katrina victims taught me a lot about how one individual can make a big impact.
- Studying in Morocco taught me to value my freedom as an American woman.
- Running a marathon to support breast cancer research put me in touch with the necessity for all of us to support one another in overcoming life's difficult circumstances.

What particular character trait do you most value in yourself and how did you discover you had this trait?

- I value my trait of compassion. I learned I had this trait when I helped an unpopular girl at our school out of a difficult situation.

- I value my integrity. I learned what it means to me when our school was rocked by news of a burglary and everyone was suspect.

- I value my sense of commitment to family and friends. I learned how much upholding my commitments means to me when my 10-year-old sister, who relied on me to take her to a series of dance rehearsals, was chosen to perform on Broadway.

Have you experienced a loss that has shaped the way you feel and think and behave?

- My best friend's brother died in a car accident a year ago, and I feel I must live for two as he was a person who had much to offer others, and I want to help fill the gap he left.

- When I moved from the neighborhood where I had gone to grade school and junior high school and entered a high school 1,000 miles away, instead of mourning my old friends, I created an online system for staying in touch and introducing them to my new friends.

- I miss my grandmother who died when I was 12. To remember her, I embroider like she did, and while I sew, I imagine conversations we might have.

What are the most meaningful ways you help others?

- I tutor grade school kids weekly so they will succeed at school even though their parents are burdened with working long hours and can't help them with homework.
- I started a food festival to help the many ethnically diverse students at our school meet and enjoy and respect each other's cultures.
- I joined the environmental committee at my school and started an education program to help others learn how to protect our environment.

If you have been involved in helping yourself or others deal with difficult life situations, what have you learned?

- I helped my friend study all during her parents' divorce, and I learned that having the support of a friend can help someone overcome family difficulties.
- Each year I help my parents organize a bicycle marathon that raises money for leukemia research. I have learned that getting together to support a good cause brings people closer and benefits the community.
- I was out of school for three months this year with an illness that required bed rest. I learned that beyond watching TV and reading, giving myself doable tasks, such as knitting scarves for presents, and being sure to commend myself when I finished one, kept me from boredom and depression.

Have you overcome a difficult obstacle and learned about yourself in doing so?

- After a virus in my shoulder led to muscle weakness, I learned I could work hard to regain my strength.

- I lost my best friend once we got to high school, because her parents refused to allow her to see anyone who was not from her religious background. I learned I could invest in making new friendships and broaden my social base.
- After my father lost his job, we had to move to a small house away from the people and activities I was involved in. I learned how to use solitude, and now I enjoy time alone.

Have you been in a situation where the right thing to do was not clear? How did you resolve the situation, and how did that affect you?

- I didn't know whether to miss school for a month and go to help my grandmother who was ill or let the family entrust her care to a stranger. When she told me that she didn't want me to fall behind in my studies, I decided to visit her every weekend even though it was a 500-mile round trip.
- One of the mothers in our car pool kept asking us to wait in the car while she did several errands on the way home from school, and we were often over an hour late getting home. I decided to tell her that I couldn't afford to be late getting home, even though I feared I'd make her angry.
- When my sister was home from a mental health institution, she began drinking heavily. My parents would be devastated if I told them, so first I worked with my sister hoping I could help her stop drinking by encouraging her to join AA.

Have you been in a situation where the right thing to do was hard or unpopular? Did you do the right thing? How did your actions affect you and others?

- When I was in a class that became unruly with a substitute teacher, I left the room and reported what was going on to the principal. The class was given detention for a month, and although I went to detention along with the group, for a while I was unpopular.

- When an unpopular girl in our class reported that some-one broke into her locker and took some money, I thought about asking if she needed lunch money that day. But I didn't do it because I was embarrassed. For days afterward, I felt bad whenever I saw her, and I have resolved to follow my charitable feelings in the future even if I feel awkward.

- I saw one of my friend's parents arguing loudly with him and threatening to beat him. Instead of looking the other way or feeling like I shouldn't come up to them just then, I decided it was more important to diffuse the anger than to be discreet. In the days afterward, my friend was too embarrassed to talk to me, but I started doing research on abusive relationships.

Perfect Phrases for Focusing on Your Desires and Goals for the Future

How have your high school career, community service, and extracurricular activities combined to prepare you for college and for meeting your future goals?

- My high school studies, community service, and involvement in extracurricular activities have prepared me for college and meeting future goals by teaching me analytic and communication skills.
- My studies, community service, and extracurricular activities have taught me how to set goals and manage my time to reach them.
- High school, community service, and extracurriculars have made me a well-rounded person who enjoys studies, helping others, and physical activity.

How have your family life and family experiences prepared you for college and meeting life goals?

- Traveling extensively with my family has introduced me to solving problems on my feet and to the skills of self-reliance.
- Living in an extended family has taught me flexibility, which will help me get along with roommates, classmates, and teachers.
- As the child of immigrants, I have developed a respect for the work ethic, and I am motivated to become a success for the whole family, not only myself.

What has involvement in an activity important to you taught you about setting goals and achieving them?

- Being involved in a band has taught me that making plans and fulfilling them are important to feeling successful.
- Taking my writing seriously has taught me that carving out time to be alone helps me set goals for myself rather than just meeting goals that others have set for me.
- Being on a sports team has helped me see that as a team player I must commit to work as hard to reach the team's goals as I do to reach my own.

Has solving an ethical dilemma led you to a career choice? What is it, and how did solving the dilemma get you interested in the particular career?

- When I helped my mother decide to go to college at age 45 even though she would have to leave my siblings and me alone four nights a week, I realized I liked the idea of coaching people to reach for their dreams.
- After I gave up cheerleading to babysit my little sister while my father was very ill, I realized I wanted to study early childhood education.
- When I didn't know how to tell my friend's parents she was using drugs, I realized I wanted to study more about how to support families where someone is ill. I became a member of NAMI, a national association that supports those who have family members afflicted with mental illness.

Have you had deep disagreements with parents and other family members about your goals for the future? What were the disagreements, and how are you addressing them?

- My family does not believe women need careers outside the home. I have addressed my desire to study by showing my parents the good that educated women do in our ethnic community.

- My family did not at first agree with my desire to study away from home. I have taken the college catalog and underlined the opportunities that exist for me as well as the school's services. I also pointed out my skill at being able to care for myself.

- My parents wanted me to follow in my father's footsteps and become an engineer who could take over the family business; however, I am interested in music. I have invited my parents not only to my concerts, but to concerts by my teachers. I have arranged conferences for my parents with my teachers so they will be assured that there is a career for me in music.

Have you lived outside the United States and attended international schools or attended many different schools for some reason or had an alternative education? How has this affected your grades and learning?

- As an army brat, I have lived in seven countries. I have learned how to make friends quickly and how to ask questions when I don't understand something because I am new.

- I have attended a school that does not use grades to evaluate students. I have had to learn to work for excellence without being judged in the traditional way.

- I have moved often during my school career, and this has caused my grades to be lower than they should be, given my abilities. Sometimes, sad at leaving a school, I refused to participate fully in the new one and sometimes, although I was participating, I did not have the same background in a subject that my classmates had.

Have you suffered deficits in your education because of your educational background?

- I attended public schools in inner-city buildings, and the lack of equipment and textbooks took its toll on my learning.
- With undiagnosed ADHD, I experienced "blinks" and missed out on much of the lessons my teachers prepared.
- I entered school in the United States when I was 12, and although I learned English quickly, I got behind in studies that required a lot of reading in English.

What are your deficits and how are you addressing them with extra courses, medication, or tutoring?

- I was not as quick with numbers as I'd like to be so I enrolled in a local business college to learn some of the basic math I think was left out of my education.
- I am working with a doctor on getting therapeutic doses of Adderall, and my focus and attention are very good. My grades have gone up considerably, as have my test scores, now that I can concentrate without becoming distracted.
- I joined a book group at our library so I am sure to read more in English and be able to discuss books in English.

Perfect Phrases for Figuring Out Why You Want to Go to a Particular School

What do you most hope to get out of your college studies?

- I hope to prepare for medical school.
- I hope to learn French and study art in France.
- I hope to network with students and professors in the field of social services.

What courses are you most excited about having the opportunity to take?

- I am most excited about the core curriculum and the way it will help me build a solid foundation for future studies.
- I am most excited about the foreign language department.
- I am very excited about the idea of studying history in a school that is steeped in the history of our nation.

What professors attracted you to a particular school and why?

- I know that Dr. Smith is considered the premier researcher in his field, and I look forward to studying with him.
- Professor Green is known for her writing, and I look forward to being in her class.
- Because the history department has been awarded a special endowment for visiting professors, I know I will have the opportunity to learn from a variety of experts.

How have you used educational opportunities and taken advantage of what your school and community offer? How do you expect that your efforts will dovetail with your experience at the college of your choice?

- I took advanced placement courses at my school, and the material we covered will help me move ahead rapidly in the college program.
- I learned how to do research by attending a community lecture series at my town's library and following up by reading the books to which the speakers referred.
- I enrolled in summer enrichment programs for two years and was exposed to college campuses in my area. I believe I have learned how to study effectively, approach professors with questions, and work with classmates to understand new material.

What clubs will be significant ones for you and why?

- Participating in band will be important to me, as I want to extend my ability with the trombone.
- As a future lawyer, I want to become involved with the school's debate team.
- Because I plan to major in medicine, I want to volunteer at the campus hospital.

What special programs attract you and why?

- Studying abroad in Norway is high on my list.
- The joint major in political science and law is very attractive to me.
- I plan to enter the business school program and make use of the special Center for Entrepreneurial Studies.

What attracts you to the school's location and how will being there help you?

- Studying in Boston means I can attend lectures at many school campuses.

- In Washington, D.C., I can clerk for government officials and experience life inside the Beltway.
- As a person raised in Los Angeles, I look forward to experiencing the four seasons when I study in Wisconsin.

Has a teacher, coach, relative, boss, community leader, or peer interested you in a particular college? How did that person spark your interest?

- My science teacher speaks highly of the importance of studying humanities, as well as science, and your school is highly regarded in both areas.
- My boss at the department store where I work has convinced me that going to school in New York will put me in touch with influential people in the fashion industry.
- My favorite aunt is a graduate of your program, and I admire her career.

Perfect Phrases for Finding Out What You Will Bring to the School You Enter and to Your Classmates

Which of your interests do you find most important?

- Skiing is the most important extracurricular physical activity I do.
- Singing for relaxation is important to me.
- Cooking for homeless people has brought me joy.

What clubs do you hope to join in college, and what roles will you take on?

- I will join the ski club and hope to be an officer in the club to ensure that many others get to enjoy good skiing opportunities.
- I will sing with the school chorus. I look forward to joining the group and helping organize concerts.
- I plan to join a community service group that supplies hot meals to the homeless and will enjoy sharing recipes and cooking techniques with the other volunteers.

What new ideas will you introduce on campus, through a club or the student government?

- I would like to introduce many ideas on reducing our carbon footprint.
- I would like to introduce the idea of across-the-curriculum instruction.
- I would like to introduce the idea of receiving independent study credit for coaching community kids.

What is your most valuable attribute as a student?

- I am organized and know how to meet deadlines.
- I am tenacious and will not let a question go until I feel I understand the answer.
- I like to read and outline what I have just read.

What is your most valuable attribute as a friend?

- I can be counted on.
- By listening, I help my friends hear themselves and think things through.
- I am happy to introduce people to one another and help people extend their network of friends.

What is your most valuable attribute as a family member?

- I am loyal to the needs of my family.
- I enjoy giving my parents gifts that show how much I appreciate them.
- I am grateful to my family members for all they have given me.

What is your most valuable attribute as a member of a group or team?

- I am loyal.
- I know how to work for the good of the group.
- I show up on time and am ready to work.

How would you introduce yourself to your roommate?

- I look forward to working hard at my studies and to having fun, too.
- I wonder what I can do to make living together fun.
- I love music and chocolate.

Perfect Phrases for Addressing Diversity of Experience

Have you traveled outside the United States?

- I have enjoyed travel to several countries in Europe.
- Throughout high school, I traveled to Nicaragua with my church group.
- Living in Southern California, I made frequent trips to Mexico.
- While Canada is one of our closest international neighbors, visiting the province of Quebec turned out to a real lesson in cultural differences.

Have you lived in other countries?

- I lived in Fiji and Germany because my mother is in the military.
- I spent summers in India with my grandparents.
- I lived in China for the first 12 years of my life.

Do you live in a multiethnic neighborhood or attend a multiethnic school?

- The student body at my school is representative of our country's blend of ethnic groups.
- My neighborhood is filled with kids whose parents are from many countries.
- When our street has its annual block party, the dishes people prepare reflect Russian, Chinese, Indian, and Mexican backgrounds.

Do you belong to school clubs or community organizations that promote diversity?

- My church youth group decided to join forces with the youth group from the Korean church across the way.
- My school's International Club holds an annual food festival.
- I have attended the annual Greek Orthodox festival in my town every year since I was five.

Are you a member of a minority or special needs group?

- I am of South Indian descent.
- Unfortunately, I spent several days of each school year in shelters for abused women and their children.
- My grandfather is one quarter Cherokee, and my family has connected with his tribe.

Are you an immigrant?

- My family immigrated to the United States from Taiwan when I was 11.
- My family came to Los Angeles from Vietnam when I was six.
- My parents brought my siblings and me from Hungary to the United States six years ago.

Are you the child of immigrants?

- My parents, who are from Lebanon, resettled in Los Angeles because they had friends there. They had me two years later.
- My parents came to the United States from Ireland because my father was working for an American high-tech company. I was born in the Silicon Valley.

- I am the youngest of five children and the only one born in the United States after my parents left Kenya.

Have you ever been the only person from your background in a group?

- Ours is the only Vietnamese family in our town, so my name sticks out on any list at school.
- The kids at my school have never teased me about my background, even though I am the only African American student at our school.
- As the only Jewish person on the committee, I had to explain why I'd prefer for our events not to be during the day on Saturday.

Do you want to study abroad?

- After studying Spanish since I was in a grade school immersion program, I look forward to a year abroad in Spain.
- I have heard that Dublin is now a wealthy city due to the high-tech work U.S. companies send there, and I would like to study in an environment that is newly thriving yet has a memory of poverty and war time.
- I look forward to the opportunity to visit Japan and study in Kyoto, where I can learn about the ancient temples and observe today's monks.

Perfect Phrases for Showing the Way You Take Initiative

Was there a problem at your school, in your community, or in your family that you identified, defined, and addressed?

- I saw that my family was growing distant because we never ate dinner together anymore, so I launched a "Let's All Eat Together No Matter How Late" evening by baking a pie and slipping invitations to come have some under everyone's bedroom door.
- I was upset that teens in my community were getting a bad name from loitering outside businesses, so I started a teen helper program to match up business owners and teens who could help them in their stores.
- When morale in my school was low after three favorite teachers left to teach in other communities, I approached the administration about holding an assembly called "The Best of ..." where students who had prepared speeches or songs or skits could honor the departed teachers and tell the school what they most missed.

Is there a new activity you created to fill a need you saw for others and yourself?

- I realized that many of us in my school were putting off studying for the SATs so I started a study group.
- I observed that although I live in a metropolitan area, my particular town is not integrated or multiethnic, so I started an International Club at school to invite guests to speak to us about their diverse communities.
- Because there are not many facilities for social activities for

teens in my town, I organized a Saturday car pool among my friends so we could use a nearby skate park, community billiards room, and state-of-the-art media center.

Was there a time that you convinced others to create something new?

- I spoke before the town's arts council and convinced the members to hold a juried youth art show each spring.
- After researching how to attract native bees to gardens, I convinced local senior citizens to build bees nest logs and give them out to community gardeners at our town's farmers market.
- By writing columns for my school newspaper, I brought student attention to how we might each help reduce our school's carbon footprint and use saved utility fees for activities.

If you could start any club or program not yet offered at the school you are applying to, what would it be, how would you start it, and why would you start it?

- In college, I would love to write a grant to start a ballet program for inner-city children to help them learn mastery and independence.
- As a college student from a rural area, I would like to use my contacts to start a lecture series on luring young people back to rural towns.
- As an enthusiastic sports participant, I would like to organize my teammates to become coaches. I would like to provide an incentive for them to coach by getting the School of Education to offer independent study credits for coaching.

Perfect Phrases for Showing Your Leadership Qualities

Have you led fundraising activities for any organization?

- I organized a UNICEF drive this year and helped trick-or-treaters in my town donate $3,000 to help children around the world.
- I was on a committee charged with raising funds for our senior trip and led in surveying the student body about fundraising activities they would most like to do.
- I am active in a group that puts on talent shows to raise money for an orphanage in India.

Have you led in creating activities for others?

- I decided that the children in my neighborhood needed more to do during the summer, so I organized a youth community theater program.
- I saw that my grandfather was growing bored now that he isn't driving any more, and I organized services to help get him out, from Dial-a-Ride to a family tree of volunteer drivers for shopping trips.
- My friends wanted to learn guitar so I found a teacher and organized group lessons, as well as a practice schedule for all of us to support one another in our endeavor.

Have you had a role in student government?

- I am an elected representative to the student council and represent the concerns of my freshman class.
- I am secretary of our school's student council and am in charge of keeping good records of our meetings and events.

- I am a member of the student council's lunchroom committee and led an effort to decrease the amount of highly salted and overly sweetened foods served to us.

Have you led a team in doing community service projects?

- Under my leadership, 15 Cub Scouts collected litter from our town's park for four Saturdays.
- I organized members of my school's jazz band to cook meals at the Veteran's Hall over Thanksgiving and give a concert for the men who were eating there.
- I motivated a group of students to create materials about household safety and emergency preparedness for distribution in our community.

What leadership roles have you taken on? What did you learn about working with others, setting goals, and the way people can make a difference?

- As captain of my school's football team, I laid the foundation for my team's success by motivating the team with rewards like coupons for free pizza for coming out and practicing over the summer. I learned that when a leader treats his team well, his team will treat one another well.
- I led my family in building a swimming pool this summer. I learned that motivating others whose hard work is required involves being a good example, pitching in, staying organized, using everyone's particular strength, and being sensitive to offering opportunities for them to learn something new.
- I wanted to see our community start an exchange program for unwanted items. I made an appointment with

one of our mayor's aides to talk about my idea, and she helped me create a network of government agencies I could approach for resources. I learned the value of having enough confidence to connect with someone who can help me.

Are you involved in athletics, competitive debating, or other competitive pursuits? How has your experience developed your ability to be a team player and/or lead a team?

- In debate team, I learned that listening closely is important to helping new members succeed.
- On the football team, I learned that leadership involves developing trust by listening and not judging.
- As a runner, I learned that I can motivate my teammates by sharing some of the tricks I've developed for staying motivated.

What's Next?

Now that you've inventoried yourself for information and an outlook you might want to apply to your application essay, it's time to match what you've thought about with the variety of question options available. We will use the six Common Application essay topics and the perfect phrases that go with them to help you write your answers. Practically all other questions on applications are variants of these questions. If you're working on applying to a school that does not accept the Common Application, convert the question, as I did earlier with the Stanford questions, into a close cousin from the Common Application list of questions (including number 6: Topic of Your Choice). Then use the following chapters of this book to help you write your essay. This goes for writing answers to the short supplemental questions and for writing addendums to your applications (see Chapter 8, Writing on the Topic of Your Choice).

Although you may skip to chapters that seem the most useful to you, reading and working your way through the pages of how to write for all the questions will help you find more and more to write about, offering you options and possibilities you might not have considered. No matter which question you choose to answer, working with Chapter 2 will prove valuable for helping you learn to collect your strongest material.

Chapter 4
Perfect Phrases for Significant Experience or Ethical Dilemma Essays

Common Application Question #1: Evaluate a significant experience, achievement, risk you have taken, or ethical dilemma you have faced and its impact on you.

Many students have had experiences that altered their lives, encouraged value setting and skills building, and helped set important life goals. Sometimes those experiences are filled with grief, such as losing a loved one, watching friends or family members deal with someone's illness, or having to move from a beloved community. Sometimes they are athletic experiences that involve training and commitment that shape an outlook. Sometimes they are church-sponsored trips and activities that have broadened views into how the world works and what the world's poor desperately need. Sometimes, they are experiences gained by working toward a fund-raising goal or policy-setting goal with others or contributing to the community with time and service.

To evaluate such an experience means to relive it on the page and draw lessons from it to illustrate how you have changed and grown. Whether or not the perfect phrases for helping you conjure your story appear in your finished essay, they will help you set your experience on the page.

Perfect Phrases for Finding Your Material as You Begin

Fill in specific details of your experience until they add up to something you want to write about:

- When I went to _____, I did _____.
- When I went to _____, I thought _____.
- When I went to _____, I said _____.
- When I went to _____, I remembered _____.

In the first part of the sentence, fill in a place you visited, an activity you participated in, or a person you saw. Next fill in what you did, thought, said, remembered to make the experience vivid and meaningful. Then write this next sentence:

- Now, I think about _____, and I put my thinking to use by _____.

And/or:

- My dilemma was _____.
- I am unhappy that I made the decision I did because _____.

Or:

- I am glad I made the decision I did because _____.

Here are some examples of what this might look like:

- When I went to New York, I walked the crowded streets for hours …
- When I went to eat after a while, I thought that living in New York could be lonely despite all the people because so many people know nothing about me.

- When I went to the main public library I had heard so much about, I said hello to a student who was seated on the floor reading note cards.
- When I went to look at what he was reading and saw that it was from an e. e. cummings manuscript, I remembered how much fun I'd had studying poetry in English class.
- Now I think about how I might have talked with the student more, and I put my self-confidence to use by not hesitating to talk to others who seem interested in what I am interested in.
- My dilemma was feeling alone and anonymous in a big, impersonal city.
- I am unhappy that I did not make the effort to speak to him. If I had spoken to him, I might have found out if he was a college student in the city and asked how he liked studying in New York.

Here's another example:

- When I went to Mexico to help build a school in a village, I did not know what poverty looked like up close.
- When I went to the town in Mexico, I thought the people there couldn't be happy because of all they don't have.
- When I went to the town in Mexico, I said I wouldn't be able to do without fresh vegetables from all over the world or a good telephone connection to use any time I wanted.
- When I went to the town in Mexico, I remembered that people can turn to each other to enjoy stories and songs they tell and sing together rather than watching a TV.

- Now, I think about how groups connect by sharing experiences and fun, and I put my thinking to use by creating games and activities for school groups to use.
- I am glad I made the decision I did because I feel more alive and involved.

And here's a third example of how you can use these sentences to help yourself find a story inside your experience:

- When I went to the state orchestra tryouts, I felt I could not possibly play well enough to make a seat in the orchestra.
- When I went to audition, I thought that I needed to keep myself from worrying.
- When I went to put my bow to the strings, I said that I was ready to play.
- When I went to draw the bow along the strings, I remembered a sunny day when I was a kid and how much fun I'd had flying a kite.
- Now, I think about how a fun, soothing day helped me play well, and I put my thinking to use by remembering I can relax when I am tense just by changing what I am thinking about.
- I am glad I decided to try out even though I didn't make a seat in the orchestra because I learned something important about how to cope when I am under pressure.

"This Is a Story about ... "

When you need to remember the images and details of an experience, it's helpful not to worry about chronology and narrative as you begin writing, because you might become stymied wondering how you'll fit everything together. In that state, you might inadvertently squelch details so you won't have more than you think you can handle. However, at the start, having more details than you can use is good. Later, you can choose from a wealth of information. If you limit yourself in remembering details, you may end up working without the most interesting ones. When you delete information too soon, you rarely arrive at the most compelling story.

Therefore, repeating the phrase, "This is a story about ... " and making a list using the details and images of your experience will provide a framework that relaxes you and allows your images to more easily come to mind.

If, for instance, you were part of an international delegation of students, you might write:

- This is a story about high school seniors who come from many countries—Japan, England, France, Canada, Brazil, Kenya, and the United States.
- This is a story about a conference room with red drapes at the Holiday Inn in Belgium.
- This is a story about some of the students liking coffee and some of them liking tea.
- This is a story about trying black tea when I usually still drink milk.

- This is a story of making a 12-hour trip and wondering if I would be able to speak with others when I arrived.
- This is a story about saying "hello" in English and not knowing what word I would hear back.
- This is a story about putting myself in situations where I have to take risks that will allow me to overcome shyness and learn more about who I am and more about the world.

Using the "This is a story about ..." phrase will help you keep writing until your list takes you deeper into the experience and you recall more particulars. Try to use the names of places and people, snippets of what you heard, and colors from the experience, among other details and images. By staying particular, you eventually arrive at some lines that evaluate the experience and let you know something of what it taught you.

After you have immersed yourself in the remembered experience by writing this way, take one of the lines and let it spark more details, going for a summing up image about why this is important to you.

- This is a story about high school seniors who come from many countries—Japan, England, France, Canada, Brazil, Kenya, and the United States.
- This is a story about learning how we are different.
- This is a story about learning how alike we are.
- This is a story about learning how I want to connect with others and share who I am, hoping I can make a difference.
- This is a story about being given a responsibility and finding out that I will hold that important responsibility for years.

Next, take one of your new lines and write more "This is a story about ... " phrases under it to show what made this impact come about. Be as specific as you can:

- This is a story about standing next to Jacques and thinking that I didn't know what to say.
- This is a story about looking at the red curtains and seeing how much they resembled the curtains in my living room at home.
- This is a story about catching myself wishing I were home eating with my family.
- This is a story about seeing Jacques looking at the floor.
- This is a story about wondering what the parquet tiles made him think about.
- This is a story about realizing that we could both be lonely or try to get to know one another.
- This is a story about saying, "Bon jour! Do you speak any English?"
- This is a story about hearing Jacques say, "Hello. Tu parles un peu de français!"
- This is a story about smiling and searching for the next words I knew in French.

Whether you are writing about winning an award, overcoming an obstacle, losing a friend or relative, or becoming proficient with an instrument or in athletics, the "This is a story about ... " litany will help you pull the details from yourself so you can put a compelling experience on the page.

Perfect Phrase: "When I ..." for Ethical Dilemma

You can do the same kind of writing a little differently by using the "When I" phrases introduced on page 54:

- When I went to _____, I did _____.
- When I went to _____, I thought _____.
- When I went to _____, I said _____.
- When I went to _____, I remembered _____.

These phrases can introduce any experience. They also work well in helping you focus on an ethical dilemma.

- When I went to see my friend, I didn't get very far in the door before I noticed he was rolling a joint.
- When I went further inside, I thought how much I dreaded having to address what he was doing.
- When I went over to sit near him, I said, "Hey, Jack, I feel bad finding out you are getting high."
- When I went home, I remembered that he had been very upset the past week because his girlfriend broke up with him.

Here are two more sentences that can help you work through how to use the experience for your essay:

- Now, I think about _____, and I put my thinking to use by _____.

And/or:

- My dilemma was _____.
- I am unhappy that I made the decision I did because _____.

Or:

- I am glad I made the decision I did because _____.

Perhaps you didn't do anything about your friend's way of coping, and he went further downhill before his parents noticed and got him help, and you feel bad that you didn't inform them sooner. Your dilemma was between snitching on a friend and getting him in trouble, or not helping others help him by withholding information. You can write about the ways you know better now by starting off, "I am unhappy that I made the decision I did because ... " If you're writing about a dilemma you solved to your satisfaction, you can draw lessons from that by writing, "I am happy I made the decision I did."

With all these phrases, the more lines you write, the more material you will have to choose from and the more interesting ideas and images will occur to you. When you are listing and not judging the value of what you're writing, you'll uncover gems that you'll put to good use in your essay. Remember, once you have the material generated, the perfect phrases you used for gathering the material may not be important enough to include in the essay, and as you cut to make word length limits, your own words will rise to the surface.

Another way to generate specific experiences to write about is to imagine a location that you can write from to tell your story. In the example of being part of an international student delegation, it could be from a chair in the conference room, from an airplane seat on the way home, or from sitting at the computer typing an e-mail to new friends.

Whatever you're writing about, in your mind put yourself in a specific place you experienced during the event you're writing about and tell others what you did from that place. Use the following perfect phrases to help you write.

Perfect Phrases for Gathering More Specific Images from Your Experience

Perfect Phrase "What I do ... "

The perfect phrase "What I do ... " results in a gathering of images and actions:

What I do on my flight home from the international conference:

- I write in my notebook about our days in the conference room.
- I remember Kyoko telling us about her mother's tea ceremonies, the way the first person to drink almost always apologizes for going before another.
- I continue making plans to find out more about U.S. colleges for Nigel from Kenya.
- I look out the window, and the clouds I see remind me of the linen tablecloths we had each day in the conference room and the way we felt important because of them, no longer just kids, but people the world really needs.

Perfect Phrase "When I ... "

The perfect phrase "When I ... " followed by the verbs such as saw, felt, listened, tasted, and smelled offers another way to gather specific images for remembering moments from the experience you are writing about. When you involve your senses, you reveal your inner thinking and feeling by "bouncing off" the sensory information you include.

Here's an example using the conference:

- When Kyoko described the impact of Hiroshima on her grandparents and their town, I felt my sweaty palm in my lap and thought about the intense heat of the blast. I listened and heard the tears in her voice, her grandparents' pain still inside of her. I tasted the tea before me with sugar in it and thought about the way Kyoko was not bitter. I smelled the starch in the linen tablecloth that covered the conference table, and I thought about how stiff we are when we become immune to the pain of others.

Once you have gathered more specific images of an experience, you are deeper into your experience. You'll be writing it on the page as if you are living it. This will make it easier to find that fresh moment of insight for yourself and your readers as you continue to write and form your essay.

After you have the images and details on the page, there are phrases that can help you find and articulate the meaning in your experience and make the insight compelling to the reader. The following phrases will help you discover more about why you are writing the particular experience you chose, and they will guide you through the middle of your essay.

Perfect Phrases for Further Researching Your Experience and Its Meaning

Consider where starting with phrases such as these take you.

- In the months following my experience, ...
- Each year as I look back on my experience, ...
- It hasn't been that long since I had the experience, but I ...
- Having this experience has changed me in these important ways:

Here are some samples from the examples I have been using:

- In the months following my experience, I have paid attention to my friend's activities and feelings. If I see something wrong, I talk to my friend and ask what I can do. If he tells me there isn't anything I can do, I suggest that there really might be. I share my ideas with him. I tell him that I am on his side and that life and health are more important to me than any momentary anger he might feel toward me.
- Each year as I look back on my experience, I feel more pleased that I stood up for what was right when I noticed two students using club money for nonclub purposes.
- I have new friends, and the International Students' Club I loved so much is serving many new students as they adapt to a new culture.
- It hasn't been that long since I had the experience, but I see that it is going to affect me for years to come. I now know the value of making sure I don't let tasks and responsibilities tumble out of control. I no longer feel bad about asking for help. I see that by asking and delegating, I am

building a stronger club and helping others build deeper ties to the organization and to one another.

- Having this experience has changed me in these important ways: I no longer leave tasks to the last minute. I approach each day with energy and commitment to getting my work done. I make sure I find the time to relax each day or have physical activity. I have a fun, in-depth conversation with a friend or teacher every day, and I make time, even if it is short, to enjoy observing nature.

Now that you have key elements and images of your experience on the page, it's time to articulate in one sentence why you're writing about what you've chosen. This sentence will guide you as you compile your essay.

This is called a *thesis statement,* and it summarizes the argument of your essay. In the case of writing from personal significant experience, it articulates the reason you're writing about this experience and what you want readers to know about you.

Perfect Phrases for Articulating Where Your Story Is Going in Terms of Insight

The Thesis Statement

- Because I _____, I know this _____.
- Since my experience, I have come to believe _____ and I plan to _____.
- After [insert the experience], I am sure _____.
- As someone who [insert a new learning or goal], I feel _____.

In the example we've been using, some thesis statements built from these phrases might be:

- Because I served as my high school's delegate to the 2007 International Students' Conference in Belgium, I have a renewed sense of purpose and dedication, and therefore, in college, I want to devote my out-of-class time to helping those in immigrant communities overcome obstacles as I learn more about their cultures and broaden my own outlook.
- Since my experience as my high school's delegate to the 2007 International Students' Conference in Belgium, I have focused my goal on becoming a foreign policy maker and future ambassador. I am excited about pursuing international studies and a year-abroad program.
- Since serving as my high school's delegate to the 2007 International Students' Conference in Belgium, I have begun a fund-raising drive in my town to help a village in Kenya grow crops.

- After serving as my high school's delegate to the 2007 International Students' Conference in Belgium, I want to join the Peace Corps after my college graduation. During college I want to spend my summers working for non-governmental organizations in emerging nations.
- As a future writer and news correspondent, I feel the time I spent at the 2007 International Students' Conference in Belgium solidified my interest in foreign affairs and helped me see how to become involved in that area while I am a student.

Your thesis statement might come at the opening of your essay, or it might be written into the middle of the essay, or it may find its place at the end. Alternatively, the statement may not appear in your essay at all even though it was a tool to help you focus on what you wanted to say and in what order. As you continue putting your experience on the page, you'll figure out where this statement belongs.

Now, if you're certain you want to write the personal experience or ethical dilemma essay, skip ahead to Part Three. Better yet, explore some other possible answers you might write for application essays by continuing to work with the perfect phrases in the rest of Part Two. Even if you don't change your mind about the essay topic you are choosing, you will have gained more practice in gathering experience for whatever you write about. The time investment is not big compared to the gain in freeing your writing self and increasing confidence in your writing.

Chapter 5
Personal, Local, National, or International Concerns

Common Application Question #2: Discuss some issue of personal, local, national, or international concern and its importance to you.

When you choose this question, choose an issue for which you can show you have been involved through reading, through activities, through organizations, and/or bringing the problem to the attention of someone who can help you make a difference. Whatever the concern—be it the plight of the children of illegal immigrants, the difficulties of single-parent families, poverty in Ecuador, the increasing death tolls on your state's highways, deaths from a particular illness, boredom among the youth of your community that leads to drug use and theft, the way racial stereotyping is increasing because of the war on terror—what you write has to show how you are involved in remedies. What you write can go further and show how you'll involve others in solutions while you're in school and beyond.

After you've noted the areas of your local or national interest and concern, use these phrases to gather information for your essay.

Perfect Phrases for Mining Your Interest in and Connection to Social and Political Issues

- **I donated money to _____.**
  - I donated money to cancer research.
  - I donated money to our local hospice.
  - I donated money to the Democratic Party.

- **I raised money for _____.**
  - I raised money for improvements to the pool at our community center.
  - I raised money for a family in town whose father was hurt when a crane collapsed.
  - I raised money among sponsors for my mother's run in support of breast cancer victims.

- **I volunteer for _____.**
  - I volunteer for the local hospital.
  - I volunteer for the local senior center.
  - I volunteer for annual beach cleanups.

- **I helped my parents in their efforts to _____.**
  - I helped my parents in their efforts to assist those who don't have health insurance.
  - I helped my parents in their efforts to educate others about emergency preparedness.
  - I helped my parents in their efforts to create a block watch program.

- **When my teacher _____, I knew I had to _____.**
  - When my teacher discussed the way hundreds of women misunderstood signs of serious illness in their

children, I knew I wanted to volunteer at our local health clinic and educate as many women as I could.

- When my teacher told our class how many children live in homes for abused women and can't go to regular school, I knew I wanted to volunteer to tutor the kids in shelters.
- When my teacher showed us pictures of plants in a vegetable garden in the middle of a city, I knew I wanted to start a community pea patch program near our school and involve children in growing food for their families.

■ **I often read about _____, and I realized _____.**

- I often read about epidemics expected in the next decades, and I realized that I want to do biomedical research to help curb them.
- I often read about the effects of global warming, and I realize that my interest in chemistry can help me contribute to solutions.
- I often read about the waste we create with our lifestyle of bottled water and packaged foods, and I realize that I want to help invent ways to deliver food to market that doesn't use energy and resource-inefficient packaging.

■ **When I fantasize about being able to change one thing about this world, this is what I imagine: _____.**
- All explosives have disappeared and people can no longer use guns and bombs to get their way.
- Suddenly, every country in the world has something of value to offer to other countries, and trading equally allows us all to live comfortably.

- Everyone alive is able to create and contribute electrical power to the world's power grid.

■ **Each summer, I have worked with [name of a government agency, hospital, or nonprofit dedicated to social action], and this has made me think _____.**

- I have had summer jobs with my local hospital, and this has made me think that, although technology has helped cure many people, everyone who works in a hospital has to remember to treat patients like they are people and not machines.

- Because I have worked for a nonprofit arts group each summer, I have learned how grants to provide seed money for artists have ensured that our community has great art in public places as well as great artists.

- I worked for my congressional representative in the summer and was exposed to social agendas, legislative discussions, and public comment. This exposure has made me think that more people need to stay involved in governing so that we can come as close as we can to a government by the people and for the people.

Now describe your activities in further detail by introducing the additional perfect phrases from the next section.

Perfect Phrases for Stating What Your Interest in a Social Issue Means to You

- **Now that I have read more widely on the topic, I . . .**
  - Now that I have read more widely on the topic of restoring salmon breeding grounds, I think towns must secure legislation to regulate building along salmon rivers.
  - Now that I have read more widely on the topic of our country's health insurance problems, I advocate universal health insurance.
  - Now that I have read more widely on the topic of race relations, I see how a country has to be ever-vigilant about equality.

- **Now that I have experience working on changing _____, I . . .**
  - Now that I have experience working on changing how my county regulates fishing, I am advocating a different licensing procedure.
  - Now that I have experience working on changing the way students in my school decide on their senior project, I see that putting alternatives up before the whole student body is best done after a committee has done some research.
  - Now that I have experience working as an assistant to a local park ranger, I want to educate the public about how everyone can help preserve open spaces for future generations.

- **Three examples of what concerns me are:**
  - Three examples of what concerns me are the depletion

of species worldwide, epidemics such as bird flu, and increasing amounts of heavy metals in fish.

- Three examples of what concerns me are the expectation that gas prices should remain low, our country's inability to withdraw troops from Iraq, and our spending to build a wall between our neighbors to the south and ourselves.

- Three examples of what concerns me are people's feelings that their vote makes no difference; their feelings that things should cost very little despite the labor, effort, and resources that go into making them; and the way people think someone else is responsible for making things happen.

After you have introduced the concern and what you are thinking and/or doing about it, you need to delve further into your subject. The next section has perfect phrases to help you fill your readers in on how the experience has helped you set goals.

Perfect Phrases for Finding a Larger Picture than Your Initial Entry Point

■ **After two years of volunteering [or donating money to or raising money for] _____, I realize ...**

– After two years of donating money to cancer research, I realize that I am ready to be a block captain and encourage others to donate.

– After two years of volunteering for the Breast Cancer Marathon and aiding runners with water and Power Bars, I am ready to do the run myself and train some friends to be support staff.

– After two years of donating money to the local Democratic Party, I want to organize an event for young new voters that will raise a lot of money.

■ **Since my parents have involved me in their efforts, I imagine taking things a step further ...**

– Since my parents have involved me in their efforts to help those who don't have health insurance, I imagine taking things a step further and helping draft a state health plan.

– Since my parents have involved me in their efforts to educate our neighbors about preparedness, I imagine holding classes for my dorm mates when I am in college.

– Since my parents have involved me in their efforts to create a block watch program, I imagine being sure my dorm mates understand how much "eyes on the street" and not leaving tempting items in full view reduce theft.

- ■ **After I learned ..., I went on to read ...**
  - After I learned about the rate of snowpack melt on mountains around the world, I went on to read national and international white papers on the subject.
  - After I learned about stunning new procedures for curing cancer, I went on to read the annual reports of the cancer center where I live, and I believe now is an exciting time to enter medicine because there is so much hope for patients.
  - After I learned that soil contains bacteria that, when breathed in, makes a person feel happy, I was even more enthused about creating a pea patch at my school, and I read about many urban gardening projects that succeeded.
- ■ **The more I learn about ..., the more I ...**
  - The more I learn about the way city kids have started businesses growing fruit and vegetables and selling them to raise money for community programs, the more I want to start this project in my town.
  - The more I learn about tutoring from the program for kids of immigrants, the more I feel the gratitude of the children and their families, and I want to help the children adapt to their new culture.
  - The more I learn about unnecessary waste in American products, the more I am committed to becoming an engineer and creating more efficient systems for manufacturing and delivery of goods.

■ **I know fantasizing about change is easier than making changes, but without imagination there is often no growth toward solving problems. My plans include . . .**

- writing a play about a time when people become incapable of using words to ignite conflicts.
- designing backpacks that are safe for young students' backs.
- creating a line of sports clothing to be made from an environmentally friendly palm tree grown in India.

After you state your plans using any of the phrases for models, you must then explain how you will carry them out. The next section has phrases for doing that.

Perfect Phrases for Citing How You Will Carry Your Interest Forward

- **During my college years, I plan to . . .**
  - run for student government and learn how policy is made.
  - write for the school newspaper and learn more about public opinion and how to sway it.
  - join the staff at the school radio station and participate in programming that brings ecological and environmental issues to the attention of everyone.
  - study educational policy so I can make changes in our country's educational ideology and method of teacher training.
  - join the International Club to meet people from many areas of the world to build a network for my future eco-friendly clothing design business.

- **After college, I hope to . . .**
  - work for the U.N. and add to my knowledge of how to use world workforces to make eco-friendly materials for packaging products.
  - go to graduate school in biochemical research.
  - study to become a doctor who can educate and treat people and stop epidemics.

- **During the summers of my undergraduate career, I will . . .**
  - help Doctors Without Borders and learn about health-care delivery during a crisis.
  - do research in my professor's lab to get a head start building up my medical research skills.
  - work for the American Cancer Society to learn about the highly functional social network that supports research.

- **One change I would like to make in my community is ...**
  - the introduction of more bulk foods for sale so people don't need to throw away so much packaging.
  - the growth of interest in replacing lawns with wildlife-friendly perennial gardens that will keep the bee population healthy for nearby farmers.
  - ending the isolation of immigrant children.

- **While I am studying in the college program, I will involve other students to help me address these concerns by ...**
  - joining the local co-op and becoming a member of its board.
  - joining the university conservation group and seeking a leadership position.
  - volunteering in local schools in the School of Education's outreach program.

Now that you have developed some writing on the topic of social concerns, take a moment to write a thesis statement. After you've written it, set it to the side as you continue developing your essay. It will act as a compass helping you make sure you are not deviating from the essay's focus. Later in this book, when we talk about openings and closings, you'll be able to make sure that no matter how colorful you get in creating an opening that hooks the reader and an ending that loops back to that opening, your essay is still focused on the topic at hand.

The next section includes two possible perfect phrases for writing your thesis sentence.

Perfect Phrases for Creating a Thesis Statement That Can Guide Writing about Concerns

- From what I know so far about _____, I believe the best way I can help work on the issue is to _____, and therefore, I am going to ...

Or

- Having been involved with _____ and seeing _____, I realize that I can make a difference by ...

Here are a few sample thesis statements on topics about social concerns:

- From what I know so far about the amount of waste in today's packaging, I believe the best way I can work on the issue is by studying engineering and devoting my career to working for a firm like Dupont, where new, nontoxic, renewable resources are being investigated. Therefore, I am going to apply to the school of engineering.

- Having been involved with young children of immigrant parents and seeing how the lack of English language skills isolates them and their families, I realize I can make a difference by studying to teach ESL. This will help me learn not only how to teach English to children but also to their parents and grandparents.

- Having been involved with raising money for cancer research and seeing the amount of public interest in finding cures, I realize that I can make a difference by going to work after college for a nonprofit fund-raising group dedicated to contributing funds to science and research.

- From what I know so far about health care in this country, I believe the best way I can work on the issue is by studying policy making and political science. Therefore, I am going to apply to the school of law, which offers undergraduate courses in these areas.

Chapter 6
Writing about a Person or Creative Work That Has Influenced You

Common Application Question #3: Indicate a person who has had a significant influence on you, and describe that influence.

Common Application Question #4: Describe a character in fiction, a historical figure, or a creative work (as in art, music, science, etc.) that has had an influence on you, and explain that influence.

If you choose to write the "influence essay," you will be focusing on how a piece of art or other work or someone in your life—a friend, boss, coach, peer, group leader, religious leader, local official, teacher, parent, grandparent, aunt, uncle, or sibling, for instance—provided you with an experience that changed the way you think and behave, or how that person became a role model for you. The perfect phrases questions in Part One may already have prompted you to think about this. Remember, an influence can be from someone you were close to who died—

the person becomes larger than life sometimes because you feel compelled to live his or her legacy.

Think about people in your life and the meaningful things they have done or said that made you stop and take note or change direction or decide to do something. Think about what you noted and what you did. Even though you must describe the influence, the most important part of the essay is how it changed you or how you decided on what is important in life because of this influence. Both parts of this essay must be filled with specific details that prove it is your story and no one else's, and they must make readers find both the influence and your behavior believable and important.

Perfect Phrases for Interviewing Yourself about Those Who Have Influenced You

Have you admired the actions or abilities of a parent, sibling, grandparent, uncle, aunt, or cousin? Who? For what did you admire this person? What character traits or attributes have you developed because of the influence of that person? What has that person taught you?

- I admire my grandfather who saved a village in India by starting reforms to subsidize the farmers. He had the courage to speak up to the government and the ability to pay attention to detail and follow through on plans. He also knew how to enlist people's trust and support and motivate them to join forces and accomplish tasks. I think the stories he told me have helped me develop those traits in my life and apply them to my school life and extracurricular activities.

- I admire my grandmother, who, at age 80, is still going to work at the print shop she and my grandfather owned together for 50 years. Her commitment to the business after my grandfather died 20 years ago taught me the importance of staying involved after a great loss. When my friend's brother died, I was able to apply this lesson by supporting him in staying involved with sports.

Have you admired the actions or abilities or words of a teacher or coach or religious leader? Who was it and for what did you admire that person? What character traits or attributes have you developed because of the influence of that person? What has that person taught you?

- "Keep working. You are doing well. You are going to live." I read those words in an essay my mother's friend wrote about regaining her strength after chemotherapy. The words of her coach at the rehab center were about more than just the exercise she was doing at the moment. Since reading these words, I have taken them on as my mantra when the going gets tough during my own gymnastics training. I have learned that positive self-talk is very effective and not only makes it possible for me to practice hard moves, but also to apply myself outside of gymnastics, as well.

- "When you bring yourself to a task, bring all of yourself," my rabbi counseled me. I was 12 and sitting in his office for Bar Mitzvah lessons. My mind was often on a girl or the amount of homework I had to do when I got home, and he could tell that my focus was scattered. I felt embarrassed and decided to figure out a way to bring all of myself to any task I was committed to doing.

Have you admired the actions or abilities of a friend or neighbor? Who? For what did you admire this person? What character traits or attributes have you developed because of the influence of that person? What has that person taught you?

- My neighbor, Mr. Getty, makes cider each year for the whole block. He invites us over to harvest apples from the many trees he has planted over the years. The next week, we press the apples into cider in an old wooden press passed down from his grandfather. Mr. Getty's house is the oldest one on the block, as the newer homes are a development made on the land his ancestors once farmed. The way Mr. Getty shares and involves his neighbors has taught me about the importance of teaching others what I know and has influenced me in starting a tutoring club at school.

■ My friend took on a paper route when he was 12. We are 17 now, and he still delivers papers mornings before school. He has used the money to invest in stocks after one of our teachers taught us some investment principles. But more than the fact that he is doing well saving for college, he says he enjoys the solitude of being outside before anyone is awake. He finds it is a good time for him to relax and prepare for the day ahead. Although I am not delivering papers in the morning, I've started to rise early and practice meditation before school.

Have you admired the actions or abilities of a celebrity or a government or social leader? Who? For what did you admire that person? What character traits or attributes have you developed because of the influence of that person? What has that person taught you?

■ I admire my town council member, John Sullivan. He has stood up for unpopular environmental legislation in our town and convinced a reluctant population of the need for regulations to preserve our town's fragile environment. Listening to him, I've learned how to convince people to do the right thing.

■ Mia Farrow's request that the government of Darfur release a political prisoner and imprison her instead made a deep impression on me. Farrow's idea led me to think about how those of us who believe in nonviolence might

help topple oppressive regimes that refuse to acknowledge human rights. Although my plan might be idealistic
and even impossible to put into action, thinking this way
has allowed me to feel that I can make a difference.

Have you admired the actions or abilities of a character in
literature or a historical figure? Who? For what did you
admire this person? What character traits or attributes have
you developed because of the influence of that person?
What has that person taught you?

- I admire Walt Whitman for his ability to celebrate life
  although he had seen awful sights and cruelty as a nurse
  in the Civil War. Reading his biography and his poetry, I
  feel a renewed sense of the importance of experiencing
  life to its fullest, and I trust in the idea that no matter how
  difficult an experience, living it will offer me the ability to
  find joy, as well.

- I admire President John F. Kennedy. His oft-quoted line,
  "Ask not what your country can do for you—ask what you
  can do for your country," mobilized the youth of the
  nation. Doing for your country meant making friends
  around the world through the Peace Corps, an organization still working today. I want to study the way words and
  phrases motivate people and use my communication skills
  to make a difference.

Have you been drawn to a piece of visual art or a particular
play, novel, poem, score, film, mathematical proof, or scientific research project? What is it, and what did it make you
think and feel? How did you change your thinking, feelings,
behavior, or goals as a result of experiencing it?

- After I read *Song of Myself* by Walt Whitman, I began thinking more about my body and the way I am connected to all that lives. Now, when I walk in the forest near my home, I notice the cedar branches reaching like a conductor's arms toward the sky. I notice the way a crane lands at the top of a fir tree, its legs trailing out below its wings like threads on my shirttail. Paying attention allows me to slow down and appreciate what is around me.

- When I saw a production of Mozart's *Don Giovanni* and focused on the statue of the father on stage while listening to the music, I felt my understanding of my relationship with my own father changing.

Once you have a piece of work or a person or a character, living, dead, real, or invented by an author that you would like to discuss as an influence, continue writing the influence essay by going on to describe the moment you saw or heard or read about the person or piece of work.

Use words that rely on the five senses so readers can feel like they are experiencing this person just as you did.

Perfect Phrases for Involving the Senses to Make the Person Real for the Reader

I watched [name of person] as [he or she] [name of action].

- I watched my neighbor, Mr. Getty, setting up the press, making sure the crank wound easily.
- I watched my town council member, John Sullivan, as he stood at the head of the room making eye contact with the audience members.

I heard [name of person] say . . .

- In a documentary, I heard John F. Kennedy delivering his now-famous phrase, "Ask not what your country can do for you—ask what you can do for your country."
- I heard a knock on our door and Mr. Getty say, "It's apple harvest time."

All around me, I felt people . . .

- All around me, I felt the class falling asleep during the film, but I was jolted awake.
- All around me, I felt people's rapt attention to the score as not a word or a cough broke the mood.

The air around me felt like . . .

- The autumn air around me felt crisp and clear.
- The air in the classroom felt refreshed by a light breeze.

Suddenly, my face felt . . .

- Suddenly my face felt rosy as if I were outdoors picking those apples.
- Suddenly, my face flushed when I remembered the times I had banged shut my bedroom door and refused to speak to my dad.

There was a taste of _____ in my mouth.

- There was a taste of earth in my mouth, like mushrooms or the forest floor.
- There was a feeling of dryness in my mouth, as I realized how wrong I had been.

And I smelled . . .

- And I smelled the heat of the stage lights.
- And I smelled the bark and leaves turning into mulch.
- And I smelled the fragrance of dogwood blossoms on the breeze.

Go on writing this scene in which someone or thing or piece of art has influenced you so the reader can experience what was happening in you. After you have the details complete, put this written essay chunk aside for a moment and write a sentence that might begin your essay.

- This past spring, my history class watched a documentary about John F. Kennedy. In it we saw him delivering his famous phrase, "Ask not what your country can do for you—ask what you can do for your country."

The sense details you wrote would follow:

- The fragrance of dogwood blossoms drifted in beneath the lowered window shades. I thought about how each spring I'd encouraged my friends to bicycle long distances on nearby trails. I realized that I want to use my persuasive skills to make a difference. Studying the way words and phrases motivate people will help me sharpen my skills and lead me to a career where I can do that.

Next, this essay could investigate classes the speaker might take to study communication skills and activities he might engage in to do that, as well. An ending to the essay could loop back to that moment where hearing President Kennedy's words and smelling dogwood blossoms brought the writer insight about himself, his skills, and how he'll use college studies to good end.

There are many more kinds of sentences you can write as focusing sentences. Following are perfect phrases for creating sentences that center a story and focus it for the Common Application question.

Perfect Phrases for Helping You Introduce the Essay as You Write about an Important Influence in Your Life

- When I was _____, I knew I was going down the wrong road but couldn't seem to do anything about it until [name of person] told me . . .
  - When I felt shy about asking teachers for special help because of my newness to English, I knew I was going down the wrong road. But I couldn't seem to do anything about it. That all changed when one teacher invited me to come in after school for some extra help.
  - When I was getting Cs in math and studying harder didn't help, I knew I was going down the wrong road. I couldn't seem to do anything about it until a coach said, "When the same box doesn't fit, try a new one." I realized that this applied to more than football strategy.

- There was a time when I didn't think I was college material, but then [who said what to you?] and I saw my potential.
  - There was a time that I didn't think I was college material, but when my English teacher praised an essay I wrote about my grandfather, who built a construction business after arriving penniless in this country, I realized I could follow his example and apply myself to reach my goals.
  - There was a time when I didn't think I was college material, but when my little brother told me how much I had taught him about soccer, I realized I might enjoy being a teacher. I asked my guidance counselor for help in researching education programs.

- I never really understood the lasting value of giving to others until [who succeeded in what area?] . . .
  - As a child who has always had whatever I wanted and needed, I understood it was good to give to others, but I never really thought too much about the lasting value of doing so until our town organized a blood drive on behalf of one of my schoolmates who had leukemia.
  - I knew my parents always contributed to our town's United Good Neighbors' fund-raising drive, but I never thought about how the money was put to use until last year when my friend's family lost their home in a fire.
- After meeting and working with [name of person], I realized who I wanted to be in this world: a person who . . .
  - After meeting and working with John Sullivan, one of our town council members, I realized I wanted to be a person who brought others together to build and maintain a solid community.
  - After meeting and working with Sally Smith, a reporter for our town newspaper, I realized who I wanted to be in this world: a person who could gather information and educate others on a large scale.
- Once I listened to _____, I was forever changed because . . .
  - Once I listened to the opera Don Giovanni, I was forever changed because I understood something important about my relationship with my father.
  - Once I listened to John F. Kennedy's speech, I was forever changed because now I was focused on what I could offer.

- **Once I read** _____, **I was forever changed because . . .**
  – Once I read Walt Whitman's *Song of Myself*, I was forever changed because I felt connected to life around me.
  – Once I read transcripts of the Senate hearing into the health risks of smoking, I was forever changed because I understood that we can go on doing detrimental things for a long time without questioning them.

- **Once I saw** _____, **I was forever changed because . . .**
  – Once I saw Mr. Getty getting his cider press out again, I knew I would in some way carry on the tradition of sharing with and teaching others.
  – Once I saw Al Gore's movie, *An Inconvenient Truth*, I was forever changed. I began to question the way I lived and what I could do to become more conscious of the way I use resources.

- **My [dad, mom, grandmother, grandfather, uncle, aunt, brother, sister, teacher, coach, religious leader, best friend] is the person who has most helped me to see who I am and what I value: [State a list of values.]**
  – My grandfather is the person who has most helped me to see who I am and what I value: perseverance, loyalty, and honesty.
  – My best friend is the person who has most helped me to see who I am and what I value: being involved, helping others achieve their goals, and learning.

- **Until I met** _____, **I believed that** _____; **now I believe . . .**
  – Until I met my best friend, Suzanne's, mother, I believed

that I couldn't become a writer. Now, I believe I can.

– Until I met John Sullivan, I thought all politicians worked only to get reelected. Now I believe there are leaders who work for the greater good.

Having introduced the person who has influenced you (or the work that has) and having stated the impact on you, build your essay further by writing about the outcome of the person's action or words. Remember to focus this way: In what way did the person (or art or piece of work) change something about you because of the impression it made?

You will have to concentrate on introducing particulars about the person who was impressive. Following are sample phrases to show you sentence patterns for achieving that.

Perfect Phrases for Evoking Particulars about What a Person Did That Was Impressive

- Ms. Taylor handled the angry customer by telling him that she wanted to help him. She then suggested that the customer tell her his top three concerns, at the same time keeping her voice warm and steady and making eye contact with the customer. I realized the value in what Ms. Taylor was doing and soon applied it to my own situation.

- When the injured boy at the skating rink couldn't get up, a concerned citizen immediately took charge, instructing one of us to call 911, another to take off his jacket and put it on the boy, and one to talk with the boy to get a name or phone number of a parent and to assure him all was going to be all right. Soon, I had an opportunity to use the organizational and crisis management skills I had admired to be sure another received help. For me the situation went this way . . .

- As a Turkish immigrant, my father started over in the United States. Unable to practice medicine as he had in Turkey, he became a physician's assistant. He looked on the bright side and enjoyed opportunities to develop warm relationships with ill people. His attitude of using what he knew to help others and our family even though he was gravely disappointed not to be seen as the respected expert made a deep impression on me and formed important life values.

- What I learned was that following through with practice and skills building is as important as being in the limelight. Even though I knew that I would spend most of my time on the bench, seriously keeping up with football practice meant that if I got put into the game, I might be able to perform an important maneuver.

■ Community service will always be an important part of my life. Taking responsibility for the welfare of others taught me the value of receiving as well as of giving, as everyone I've helped has wanted to give me something in return, if only a smile and kind words.

■ I am grateful for the lessons I learned from ballet because I am now someone who admires grace and beauty and the work it takes to achieve something that seems effortless.

Any outcome that demonstrates the development of particular character traits and moral integrity, intellectual interests, athletic interests, hobby interests, musical interests, art interests, or the strength to follow a certain direction is right on target. Any way that you can show how this learning will benefit you in college and in a career is worthwhile, as are statements about how you deal differently with friends, family, fellow students, and coworkers.

Following are the perfect phrases that will help you articulate how you will apply what you have experienced and learned in college and in your future.

Perfect Phrases for Articulating How You Expect to Apply What You Have Learned from This Influence

- I expect to thoroughly enjoy my college studies because now I have developed the maturity and study skills I need in order to excel.
- I expect to thoroughly enjoy my extracurricular activities in college because I have learned to handle myself in groups.
- My family and teachers have noticed a difference in me. They tell me I am a trustworthy and steadfast person, and they are pleased by my commitment to others. I enjoy their recognition.
- When I work with my fellow students now, I always remember to compliment them on what they are doing well. That helps motivate them to continue contributing to our effort.
- In serving my community, I realize that one person does make a difference. When I see Johnny, who was an angry loner, helping a younger child tie his shoes, I feel I have made an important difference. Because of this, I plan to study early childhood education and train parents and preschool teachers.

Now that you have phrases to help you conjure the details, images, and events of your essay about the person or work that influenced you, you can write a thesis statement. It should sum up the essay you see evolving and act as a guide or checking tool as you write so you can be sure you made and supported a strong assertion with images and details.

Again, the thesis statement may or may not end up in your essay, but it shows you what you have to cover, in what order to cover it, and what strategy to use for writing the essay. Usually for the influence essay, you use a cause-and-effect strategy. The actions of the influential person or the structure and impact of the piece of work are the cause of an effect on you. The influence changed something in you or helped you commit to something. The particular changes are the effect. The writer's job is to convince the reader that both the influence and the effects are real and that the effects make the applicant desirable to the college.

Perfect Phrases for Creating the Thesis Statement for the Influence Question

- **I know that [who or what] has greatly influenced me because I now [do or think or plan to what].**
  - I know that listening to John F. Kennedy has greatly influenced me because I have now chosen political science as a college major, and I have researched the college catalog for electives I'd like to take.

- **Whenever I hear [or say or read or remember] the words [name them], I am grateful to [name the influence on you], and I promise myself I will continue to [name the goals or action you will take as a result of that influence].**
  - Whenever I chant the words, "Keep working. You are doing well. You are going to live," I am grateful to my mom's friend for writing about her experience, and I promise myself that if she could help regain her life using those words, I can use them to work hard in my gymnastics practices and believe in my abilities.

- **There is no more profound influence on me than [name the influence] because knowing [person or work] changed my life. I am no longer someone who [name old trait or behavior] but a person who [name new trait or behavior].**
  - There is no more profound influence on me than my friend because by understanding how I helped him when he was grieving for his brother, I am no longer someone who might make a difference in the future but someone who is making a difference now.

Anything you involve yourself in can be an influence. Therefore, as you work on this essay, you might want to reread the chapter on writing about an important personal experience or ethical dilemma and use some of those perfect phrases to help you describe the person or work you are claiming as an influence.

Chapter 7
Writing for the Diversity Questions

Common Application Question #5: A range of academic interests, personal perspectives, and life experiences adds much to the educational mix. Given your personal background, describe an experience that illustrates what you would bring to the diversity in a college community, or an encounter that demonstrated the importance of diversity to you.

If you are an immigrant to the United States, the child of immigrants, or someone whose ethnicity is a minority in the United States, you might find this question an interesting one to show how your background will add to the mix of perspectives at the college you're applying to. If you're applying after having an unusual post-high school experience, such as joining the military, becoming part of a dance troupe, or caring for an elderly relative, you can use your experience to evoke the way in which you will bring diversity to campus. Or, of course, you can use the material from question 1, the unusual experience.

Writing for the Diversity Questions

If you're a minority, your family's culture and traditions and the way they have helped you develop particular character and personality traits will be of interest here. Perhaps you've grown up with a strong insistence on respecting elders, attending family events, or learning your parents' native language and culture. Perhaps you are close to grandparents and extended family who have taught you how teamwork can help everyone survive. Perhaps you have had to face and deal with difficulties that stem from your parents' values conflicting with those of your peers. Perhaps teachers have not always understood the elements of your culture and how they pertain to your school performance. Perhaps you have experienced discrimination and formed your values and personality traits around your success in spite of the discrimination.

Understanding what it means to live in two cultures and understanding how that builds empathy for others and strong will and character is a good focus for this question. If you want to use overcoming not knowing English when you started school in the United States, you might do well to use the question about significant personal achievement. If you want to evoke the flavor of a minority culture and its traditions and how they have hindered your progress in school and socially, as well as enhanced it, this is the question for you to answer.

If you're not from a minority ethnic background but have traveled a lot, hosted an international exchange student, done volunteer work in your community or in South or Central America, or belonged to the International Club at your school and learned from students of many cultures, this may be the question for you to answer, as well. If you grew up in a racially and ethnically integrated neighborhood, your growing up and experience with kids of many cultures is also a good subject for this question.

The way this question is phrased, anyone who has had an encounter based on ethnicity or race could center an appropriate essay on the experience and its aftermath concerning your thinking and resolve to educate others about diversity.

What the admissions committee is looking for here is this: Its members want to be convinced that the student body will benefit from including you because of your background. They also want to know the way your background will shape your contributions to the campus and students' learning about diverse backgrounds. If you're not of an ethnic background but have lots of cross-cultural experience, they want to see you as someone the school can count on to participate in diversity programs and build bridges between students and communities. In any case, the committee will be interested in what you can bring to your classmates and professors that addresses tolerance, making connections, and increasing long-term commitments to global understanding.

These are big notions, but the proof that you are the kind of person interested in these areas is in the details of your personal experience. You don't have to take on the world to prove that your experience will help you and others in the world. All you have to do is delve into your experience to date and write about what you know about yourself because of it.

The next section provides phrases to help you get started putting diversity experience on the page.

Perfect Phrases for Getting at the Heart of the Diversity Essay

■ I grew up in a neighborhood where . . .
  – I grew up in a neighborhood where children of five ethnic groups played together.
  – I grew up in a neighborhood where the residents spoke Spanish and could conduct all their business in that language.

■ In my grade school, I was the only kid from a _____ background. Being different meant . . .
  – In my grade school, I was the only kid from a Croatian background. Being different meant that people assumed that I didn't understand what they were saying.
  – In my grade school, I was the only kid from an Indonesian background. Being different meant that my teachers were always building a lesson around me.

■ As a high school student, I traveled to Nicaragua with my church group to help build housing for poor families. I learned an enormous amount about the ways in which people show gratitude to one another and learn from one another.

■ My parents and I came to this country from Taiwan when I was 11 years old. From the time I entered school here, I experienced a clash between the values of two cultures and had to forge my own individual identity in both of them.

■ I wouldn't trade my childhood experience of living [where] for anything. It taught me [personality and character traits].

- I wouldn't trade my childhood experience of living in Siberia for anything. It taught me the value of listening to my own thoughts and the way those who face harsh nature build strong and caring bonds.
- I wouldn't trade my childhood experience of living as the only white kid in an Asian neighborhood. It taught me to overcome feelings of self-consciousness and the skills of lowering social barriers between people.

■ Belonging to a minority culture has had definite effects on my school performance. [List them.]

- Belonging to a minority culture has had definite effects on my school performance: The teachers avoided calling on me. I believe it was because they didn't think I knew the answers.
- Belonging to a minority culture has had definite effects on my school performance: I was so preoccupied with hiding the things my mother sent with me to school that I didn't pay attention to lessons.

■ When I was in high school, I was an exchange student to [country]. I learned not only about the foreign culture I was living in but also about my own culture, which I had never had to think about so deeply before. Here is what I learned:

■ I joined the International Club at school because I wanted to host an exchange student's yearlong visit to our town. Here's what I learned:

■ I attended an English-speaking international school in Belgium where my father was working for a chemical company. My classmates were from the Middle East, Africa, and all over Europe. We traded music and jokes, clothing, and food. Here's what a typical day was like:

- My grandparents live with my family. We are sponsoring their green cards and residency in this country. They come, as my parents did, from _____. These are the customs and traditions they brought with them:

- I will never forget the confrontation between _____ and _____ and the way it taught me about the hard work involved in learning to understand one another.

- Learning a culture new to me by encountering it head on as an exchange student with no friends or family to distract me has changed my idea about cross-cultural learning.

When you know what experience you're going to write from or even if you're still looking for your focus, there are more types of phrases that can help you find the details and images to make your story compelling and real. Here are some models.

Perfect Phrases for Putting Culture Clashes on the Page

- It may seem like wearing blue jeans and drinking coffee are far from deviant activities, but when you are raised in a household that originates from [name of place], these all-American actions are considered disappointing and disrespectful.

- I kept quiet when the teacher suggested that because my family was from Iran, I would want to wear the traditional burka during the International Day food fair. She didn't understand that . . .

- I didn't know how to respond when classmates and neighbors who saw me during school hours now stared at me because I was wearing traditional dress.

- This is what my father said when he heard I wanted to attend college:

- My parents have always wanted me to pursue a career in medicine because in their culture doctors are revered. Having been raised in _____, I am drawn to study _____. In explaining my choices to my parents, I learned a lot about what they sacrificed for me.

- My classmates never really understood why I wasn't allowed to join them on Friday nights at the football field or why I couldn't eat the food in our school cafeteria.

Perfect Phrases for Describing What You Are Fond Of in Your Culture

- My parents believe I must learn the language and customs they grew up with so I can carry them on when I marry and raise children. Although I didn't want to attend the after-school program they sent me to, it wasn't long before I realized how happy I was to learn customs and language that helped me connect with my parents and grandparents.

- I find that large differences between my culture and the American culture I live in cause me to value my culture for the way it _____. In the United States, many families _____, but I was raised to _____.

- Grandma always said _____; her wisdom comes from growing up in _____. In that life, she _____. I am fond of the way she _____, and I plan to bring this understanding with me in all I endeavor to accomplish.

- I remember one particular evening when my mother said I could have a friend over for dinner . . .

- Here is what I look forward to when my extended family gets together:

- This is what I miss now that my family has moved away from my grandparents, uncles, aunts, and cousins:

- Here are the parts of my culture I continue to practice although I now live far from the country I was born in:

- My favorite holiday celebration is _____ . On this day, people in my culture . . .

Perfect Phrases for Describing Discrimination

- I had no idea why _____ was saying _____.
- When I leave my multiethnic neighborhood for extracurricular activities, I experience attitudes and interactions that never fail to surprise me.
- When I came to the United States and entered fifth grade, I did not know English. My classmates had no way of knowing that I had been a straight-A student in Ukraine or that my parents had both been scientists there.
- My classmates and teachers frequently make assumptions about me based on my skin and hair color.
- When I heard students at my school saying _____, I realized it would be a good idea if a club or class could sponsor a forum to discuss _____. I helped bring this about by _____.
- Here is a description of me made from stereotypes that people have applied to me. Here is my description of myself as I experience myself. Here is how I have helped people know me rather than apply the stereotype they have learned.

Perfect Phrases for Describing How Feeling Like an Outsider Develops Character

- When I visited _____, I was no longer part of a majority culture. At first I experienced discrimination since I was an outsider. [Provide examples.] Eventually, I realized I might be able to connect with others despite our differences. To begin this process, I _____. The results outside and inside myself were big. I found that . . .

- When you don't understand much of the language you hear around you, you become a good observer of other forms of communication. [Cite examples.]

- Now that I have acculturated, I understand how to extend myself and provide encouragement and help to others who are new to this culture.

- As an exchange student, I was suddenly cut off from the groups who knew me, and I had to learn how to feel my own self-worth without the encouragement of friends and family.

- Forced to hang around with students who were not popular with others, I began to identify what it takes to build one's self-esteem and accomplish something.

- Because I excelled in math and this subject doesn't rely knowing a lot of English, I earned the esteem of my classmates. I began to tutor them and received opportunities to practice my English.

- Since I couldn't study in English, I decided to develop my musical and athletic abilities and participated in orchestra and volleyball. I attended all rehearsals and practices and worked on my skills at home. It wasn't long before I was admired for my skill and ability to help others do well.

Perfect Phrases for Talking about the Value of Cross-Cultural Experience

- I grew up [your ethnic group] in a multicultural neighborhood. This meant that I was introduced to [describe/name a philosophy or way of living] at an early age. This became important because ...

- Because I lived in many countries during my school years, I understand how people think differently across cultures but have many of the same values. Here are several examples:

- When I was in [country], I noticed [name a custom or way of interacting]. By practicing this custom myself, I learned [name something you know about people or getting along with others now]. [Give examples of practicing the custom and how it changed you.]

- My best friend's family is from [country]. Whenever I visit my friend's home, I come away with new ideas about [learning, creativity, family life, music, food]. These new ideas are important to me because ...

Perfect Phrases for Talking about How Cross-Cultural Experiences Help One Set Goals

- Before [cross-cultural experience], I could not have imagined becoming a [career or activity]. Now, I _____. Here is how this change came about:
- Because I have experienced the difficulty of getting medical care and other services in a non-English-speaking neighborhood, I have decided to devote my career to …
- After my year abroad, I realized that …
- After I spent time visiting my relatives in [country and region], I felt drawn to becoming involved in [activity or career].
- At college, I plan to [name an activity] so I can stay in touch with my cross-cultural experience.
- I want to use my cross-cultural experience to help those new to the United States as they enter college. I plan to do this by …

Whichever of these phrases sparks a way into the essay for you, you will have to supply vivid details to continue to hook the reader into your experience and to give him or her something of the diversity you understand. Remember the phrases earlier in the chapter that helped you dig into your experience and find the details you'll want to share.

Following are additional things to search for that will help you bring your experience to life on the page.

Perfect Phrases for Gathering the Details of Your Diversity Experience

Here are some ways to capture your diversity experience:

- Name foods that are common on your family's table or the culture you have visited.
- Name articles of clothing particular to your ethnic background or the country you visited.
- List nicknames and common phrases from your native language or the language of the country you visited.
- List holidays and how they are celebrated—with what activities and what foods and why.
- List some common sayings from your culture or the culture you visited.
- Name the most important values of your culture or the culture you visited.
- List some heroes from the culture and explain why they are heroes.
- List forbidden behaviors.
- List behaviors that are encouraged or mandated.
- Describe yourself participating in an event in the culture you're writing about. Talk about what you do, see, hear, smell, taste, and touch.
- Describe a cultural strength from your background that you carry inside you.
- Describe a way you'll use that strength to help others.
- Describe a way that strength will help you succeed.
- Examine your family tree and what it has taught you about your place in history.

Look at the material you've generated by using the phrases in this chapter. Think of a scene that would evoke the culture you're writing about or the discrimination you've experienced or observed. Now start a paragraph with one line of dialogue from that scene in which you're saying something or someone is saying something to you. Before you finish the sentence, though, tell who is speaking and what he or she is doing, and describe the surroundings. Go on to write using what you've generated with the earlier phrases. When you feel you're at the end, write the finish to the scene you opened with the dialogue, adding your thoughts.

Here's an example of how I would build such an essay:

■ "What I am trying to bring out," my grandmother said, suddenly switching to English, "is that no one should have to starve in this country." As she spoke about the poor family down the street, she was cooking her famous potato blintzes to bring to them. I knew our family did not have a lot of money, but food was plentiful because my grandmother knew how to cook delicious dishes from basic ingredients.

After this paragraph, I could go on to write about the family coming from Russia, the way I watched my parents rebuild their lives by taking menial jobs when once they had been professionals. I could write about the reason for the family's move to the United States—perhaps to avoid religious persecution or to seek better educational opportunities for their children or to have access to medical care that someone in the family needed. Next, I could write about what life was like for me in a new culture, the way I had spent too much time thinking about what I couldn't do as a stranger in a new school. I could write about the way my grandmother's confidence that she could help by doing what she did best—cooking delicious food—gave me courage about my ability to contribute in my life.

To close the essay, I might write this:

- In what seemed like a few minutes, the first batch of blintzes was ready. I smelled the onions and chicken fat mixed with the potatoes and was suddenly very hungry. "It's your job to take these to the Joneses while they are still warm, Ida. Their little boy needs some meat on his bones." She handed me the plate of 12 blintzes, 2 for each one in the family. I hurried to deliver them, grateful for the food I would share with my family when I got back home and grateful for the lesson my grandmother taught me that afternoon. I was already dreaming of using my gymnastics ability to help children, especially those who weren't doing well in school.

Perfect Phrases for Writing the Diversity Essay Thesis Statement

You may think you've written a finished essay using the ideas and phrases in this chapter. However, to help you maintain coherency and focus, write a sentence that encapsulates your essay's argument or your gaining insight and what you want others to know about you because of your experience. As always with a thesis statement, the sentence may or may not appear in your essay in the beginning, middle, or end, but it will tell you how to organize the essay, what you are building toward, and how you are going to do it.

Complete one of the following thesis sentence phrases based on the story you've started developing with the phrases suggested earlier. The sentence will guide you in knowing what information to supply to the reader and what turns to take in your essay to support the argument your thesis statement summarizes.

- **As a [name ethnic group], I have experienced [what] and now I contribute to others in ways that include . . .**
  - As an Asian American, I have grown up with very high family expectations. Now I contribute to others in ways that include meeting high goals.
  - As the child of Mexican laborers, I have experienced the sacrifices my parents made to send me to school in the United States. Now I contribute to others in ways that sometimes include sacrificing immediate gratification.
- **Because I live in two cultures, I have experienced clashes and, in resolving them for myself, have grown as a person in these significant ways:**

- Because I live in two cultures, I have experienced clashes and, in resolving them, I have grown as a person in these significant ways: I am independent, keep my own counsel, and remain committed to goals.
- Because I live in two cultures, I have experienced clashes and, in resolving them, I have grown as a person in these significant ways: I understand that moving forward with my life may mean leaving old connections behind. I also understand that bringing what I value from the past into my life today makes me strong.

■ **Having experienced life in a foreign culture, I have come to understand _____ and see the value in _____.**

- Having experienced life in a foreign culture, I have come to understand that people's beliefs, behaviors, and ways of thinking are rooted in traditions. I see value in studying these cultures in order to improve world communication.
- Having experieced life in a culture different from the one in which I was raised, I have come to appreciate that the same gestures and words can have different meanings for different people. From this experience, I appreciate the value of cross-cultural training.

■ **My background carries great meaning for me, including _____, and I look forward to giving back to the society that has helped to form me by _____.**

- My background carries great meaning for me, including living by the rules of Confusionism. I look forward to giving back to the society that has formed me by helping to establish strong ties between China and the United States.

– My background carries great meaning for me, including the Jewish idea of *mitzvah*, acts of human kindness. I look forward to giving back to the society that has formed me by creating and running a college club that encourages performing mitzvah, such as taking notes for ill students and shopping for food for them.

Chapter 8
Writing on the Topic
of Your Choice

Common Application Question #6: Topic of your choice.

Just as the Common Application includes a "topic of your choice" question, it's also not uncommon for non-Common Application colleges to include this question as a choice. Yale University requires an essay limited to 500 words in its supplement to the Common Application: "While we leave the topic of your second essay entirely up to you, we encourage you to use this opportunity to tell us something that we could not learn from the rest of your application. Try to pick a topic that will convey some aspect of your experience or outlook that you would like us to understand better."

It's hard to think of an essay, including Yale's second, for which selecting one of the first five questions on the Common Application wouldn't provide an appropriate and thought-provoking prompt. It seems that any hobby, travel experience, friendship, or leadership experience would be well described using the significant experience or achievement question or the influence question. Remember, the admissions committee members want to see self-reflection in your essay, and the first five questions help you spin your essay toward insights about yourself.

If, however, no other question helps you write about (1) important life-shaping special needs, (2) particular reasons why your academic performance does not fairly represent your true abilities, or (3) an unconventional precollege background, you might want to work with the "topic of your choice" option. In this case, writing the thesis statement is of paramount importance because the question itself offers no real starting point.

Writing the thesis statement will help you find a way to organize your argument, whether it's why a particular school is the right match for you, how your academic performance was affected by circumstances beyond your control or by ones you didn't know how to control, or what has so far prepared you or led you to want to enter an undergraduate program after a gap from high school.

Before you choose this "any topic" question as your main essay, check to see if the application you're writing for has a special place for addressing issues of poor previous academic performance and/or a "why this school" supplemental question.

You can call the admissions office and ask if the admissions committee accepts addendums with the application, should you want to address special needs or explain something about your academic performance. If the answer is yes, use this chapter to help you write the short answer, supplemental answer, or addendum. Use a different one of the six questions for your main essay.

Warning: Don't use this option for submitting a paper you wrote for school, unless the school you're applying to asks specifically for one of those, and then of course, it would not be in answer to Common Application question #6. Remember that admissions committees want to get to know you, as if you were in the room with them, relating to them, not as if they were watching you relate to your classmates or teachers or giving a lecture at school.

Perfect Phrases for Writing about Special Needs or Reasons for Lower-than-Expected School Performance

- I live with [syndrome, condition], and despite [symptoms, specific difficulties or impacts] I have accomplished much, including _____. However, I know I require _____.
  - I live with diabetes type I, and despite my need to monitor my exercise, diet, and food intake, I accomplish a lot each day, including keeping up with a physically demanding after-school job at a local day care center. However, I know that I require rest during the day and a schedule that accommodates that.
  - I live with two deaf parents, and because I am the only hearing person in the family, there are many demands on my time. Even though I am the one who makes and takes important phone calls and negotiates with everyone from the landlord to the social worker, I have accomplished much, including a straight-A average and winning a spot in our school's chamber orchestra. I am eager to go to college near my home so I can continue to help my parents while I study.

- As the child of [immigrants, parents who are impaired, the foster care system], I have routinely missed out on study time because I have had to _____. I know, however, that I am prepared for college because I have [finished make-up courses, nongraded accomplishments, community service which demanded academic skills].

– As a child of the foster care system, I have routinely missed out on study time because the place I live is home to eight other children ages 2 to 17, and I am often babysitting. I know, however, that I am prepared for college because when I must perform on-the-spot writing compositions about my experience, I do well. I anticipate more study time when I am living in a dorm, and I plan to score high on all tests and quizzes.

– As the child of immigrants, I have routinely missed out on study time because I have had to work to help support my family. Although low quiz scores have brought down my grade point average, I know I will do well in college, because when I have had enough prep time before major tests, I always score above 95%. My parents have agreed to help me take out a loan so I can reduce my work hours when I am in college, and now that my older sister is working, her income will take the place of mine.

■ **Because I am so actively involved in [national athletic competition, care of a sibling or parent, the film industry, other work or social obligations that impinge on school attendance], I have often missed tests [or study time or other classroom activities]. To prepare myself for college, I have made up for this by _____.**

– Because I am so actively involved in professional theater, I have often missed tests and study time. To prepare myself for college, I have enrolled in online vocabulary and math courses, which I can do on my own schedule, and I have been scoring 3.7 or above on the weekly tests.

– Because I am so actively involved in my religious youth group, I have often missed out on extracurricular activities. I have made up for the social time I miss with school friends by inviting them over to my house for meals on weekends. I see that finding alternative ways of interacting keeps me in the loop when I cannot take advantage of structured activities.

When there is a lack of English skills:

■ English is my second language, and I didn't speak the language at all until I entered the U.S. school system in [date]. Though I didn't perform well on tests and written work at first, I gradually pulled up my grades. My recent performance indicates that I will do well in college.

■ As I learned English, I enrolled in a study skills class, which prepared me for future academics and social interaction with teachers and students.

Perfect Phrases for Writing about an Unconventional High School or Post-High School Educational Experience that Lowered Your Grades

- **There is a gap in my education because I earned my GED while I was _____.**
  - There is a gap in my education because after I was diagnosed with mononucleosis, I missed so much of my junior and senior years that I dropped out of school. While classmates finished their senior year, I worked as a cook at a local restaurant. When they all left for college, I realized what I was missing and enrolled to earn my GED while continuing to work.

- **I decided to live in [name of place] after high school to gain experience in _____.**
  - I didn't finish high school with my class because after being an exchange student to Argentina, I decided to spend a year traveling around South America to become fluent in Spanish. When I returned home, instead of enrolling in my high school and joining the class a year behind me, I tutored people in Spanish and earned my GED.

- **Because of an illness that [tell the impact of the illness on you], I had to finish my high school diploma using a special program, which [discuss the reason you didn't do as well as you might have in school].**
  - Because of an illness that required extensive bed rest, I had to finish my high school education using a special

at-home program, which did not work well for me for two reasons: I like learning among others where I can exchange information and ideas, and the program relied on rote learning, which is meaningless to me and I was uninspired.

■ **I don't have a high school diploma because _____. However, I am ready for college and have been encouraged by _____ to apply.**

– I don't have a high school diploma because my family evacuated from Iraq two months before I would have graduated from high school there. I have taken college placement tests rather than enroll for an additional year of high school.

– I don't have a high school diploma because my family relocated after Hurricane Katrina devastated our neighborhood. Our schools' records were destroyed as were the records I had at home, but my grades were always good. Now that we have settled permanently in Alabama, I am applying to college on the strength of my placement tests.

■ **I have verified my academic ability after receiving poor high school grades by attending community college courses. I took _____ and received grades of _____. Preparing for college in this way has taught me _____.**

– I have verified my academic ability after receiving poor high school grades by attending community college courses. I took remedial composition and math and received grades of 3.5 and 3.6, respectively. Preparing for college in this way has taught me that when I am motivated, I learn easily.

- ■ **My high school years were tumultuous because
  _____ and my performance was affected; however, I am preparing for my college studies by completing [name preparatory summer program or supplemental help] to ensure that I do well.**

  – My high school years were tumultuous. During my sophomore year, my sister ran away from home, claiming the FBI was after her. She was diagnosed as bipolar and institutionalized. My parents visited her every day at the facility 60 miles from where we live, leaving me in charge of my 10-year-old sister. My school performance was very much affected as a consequence of my worry and my increased responsibilities at home; however, I am on an even keel now, and I will prepare for my college studies by taking summer courses at our local community college to ensure that I do well academically.

- ■ **I had a hard time believing I would get the opportunity to attend college because _____, and the discouragement I experienced led to poor performance. However, because I [provide quantitative proof of academic ability—IQ test scores, outside-of-school scores, particular class scores from areas in which your interest overcame your sense of discouragement], I am sure I can do well in college.**

  – I had a hard time believing I would get the opportunity to attend college because my father's business failed and my parents were inundated with bills, and the discouragement I experienced led to poor performance. Now I have qualified for financial assistance and want to attend college. Because my grades have been consistently high since that news, I am sure I can do well in college.

Using the Topic of Your Choice for Writing the "Why This Particular School" Essay

Notes: Sometimes, as in the case of Sarah Lawrence College ("What about Sarah Lawrence most appeals to you?"), Trinity College of Arts and Sciences at Duke ("If you are applying to Trinity College of Arts and Sciences, please discuss why you consider Duke a good match for you. Is there something in particular at Duke that attracts you?"), or The William States Lee College of Engineering's Leadership Academy application ("Why do you want to be a part of the Leadership Academy?"), the "why this school or program" question is a required supplement to the Common Application essay. In these cases, you would of course choose a different topic for the main essay and use the following perfect phrase ideas for the supplemental essay.

Before writing a "why this particular school" essay, be sure to read the school's mission statement or description of the kind of students it wants and how it wants to foster them. With the school's wording and your knowledge of their goals in mind, you'll have a better chance of showing that you're acquainted with the school and that what you've learned about the school truly resonates with you.

For instance, Stanford University uses wording that speaks of the institution as a leader in teaching and research. Its motto, the words of president John Hennessy, is prominent on its Web site:

> "The wind of freedom blows" is an invitation to free and open inquiry in the pursuit of teaching and research. The freedom of scholarly inquiry granted to faculty and students at Stanford is our greatest privilege; using this privilege is our objective.

Writing on the Topic of Your Choice

With these words in mind, your essay about why Stanford is the school for you would emphasize your interest in free inquiry—not by parroting the words of president Hennessy, but by showing what learning opportunities you will involve yourself in at Stanford, how the location, other students, campus programs, and professors will benefit you and what you will bring to them.

Perfect Phrases for Using the Topic of Your Choice for Writing the "Why This Particular School" Essay

■ My father [mother, brother, grandparent, aunt, uncle, teacher, mentor, older neighbor] went to your university, and I am drawn to experiencing the studies, activities, and outlook they experienced.

– Based on what my mother, who is an alumna of your school, has told me, I believe I'll enjoy being an active and useful member of your college community.

– After visiting the campus and reading the catalog and online discussions about the school, I know that [particular program] is a good match for me because it will allow me hands-on learning in a supportive environment of peers and professors.

– I have dreamt of attending [name of school] since I was a freshman in high school, and my aunt gave me her college pin from the years she attended in the 1960s. I keep in touch with campus events by visiting each year and attending classes, as well as by reading my aunt's alumni news magazine.

■ I am particularly fond of the area of the country where [name of school] is located. I believe living and making connections there will facilitate my studies and involvement with supportive organizations. [Go on to show how the location will do these things for you.]

– I am particularly fond of the Boston area, and I believe that attending BU will allow me to become involved in several of Boston's historic outreach programs, as well as hear lectures by scholars and historians visiting the many campuses in the area.

– I look forward to living in Los Angeles and learning the film business. I believe that attending Loyola Marymount and becoming involved with the film school will offer me internships that will lead to a job in film production.

■ **I know my studies will involve graduate work and I believe that attending [name of school] will facilitate my entry into the graduate program I desire. [Go on to discuss particular programs, courses, exchanges, clubs, and special majors available at the college that you will find useful.]**

– I know my studies to become a lawyer will involve graduate work and I believe that attending UCLA will best prepare me for entering a medical law program. I intend to earn a double major in political science and healthcare administration.

– As a pre-med major, I will use my undergraduate studies to prepare me for medical school. Tufts' program will allow me to study deeply in the humanities, as well as the sciences, and I will enjoy having proximity to hospitals in which I can shadow physicians.

■ **When I read [name of school's] mission statement, philosophy, and course offerings, I knew that attending [name of school] would prepare me well for a productive life in which I [state what you want to do with your life]. [This essay should go on to quote the school's mission statement and educational philosophy, and demon-**

strate how you interpret their meaning in college life. Specific details about courses, activities, and community service will make this kind of essay vivid rather than general and dull.]

– When I read Trinity College's mission statement, philosophy, and course offerings, I knew that attending Trinity would prepare me well for a productive life in which I plan to enter the foreign service. "Providing a liberal environment where independence of thought is highly valued and where staff and students are nurtured as individuals and are encouraged to achieve their full potential" describes what I want in the college I attend. Trinity College's commitment "to disseminate its knowledge and expertise to the benefit of the City of Dublin, the country and the international community" is reflected in the number of campus social service organizations and the many international guest professors who teach each year.

■ [Name of school's] approach to scholarship is in line with how I learn best. [Go on to paraphrase the approach and show how you have already demonstrated an ability to thrive under such an approach.]

– Colorado College's approach to scholarship is in line with how I learn best. On the Web site, college president Richard F. Celeste writes, "Perhaps you will choose to work on a student/faculty collaborative research project, or create your own independent study. You certainly will begin the process of shaping your own direction and destiny." In high school, I thrived in courses where teachers focused on group projects and

> in those where I created my own research projects. Collaborative learning and self-directed learning motivate me because I have a stake in the results.

Alternatively, you might want to start with a quote by someone who has spoken highly of the school or someone you read or listened to at a campus visit or recruiting session. Then state the meaning of the quote to you:

■ From the moment I heard the dean say, "Strike a fine balance between flexibility and focus," I knew I would fit well in this undergraduate student body. All through high school, I have benefited from the ability to choose electives that fit my particular academic plans, and I hope to continue doing so in college with combinations of lectures, independent study, and community service.

You can start with a scene in which someone who is a role model for you is teaching, performing a task, or helping someone. Go on to show how you believe his or her traits are the result of educational experience at the school you want to attend. After a short description of that person in the situation you're observing, say:

■ I believe that [name of person's] ability to _____ is a result of studying at [name of school] and having been a member of a community that is [name a trait like compassionate, community-service minded, politically sophisticated, or egalitarian—whatever attracts you to the school]. I believe I will benefit by attending [name of school] because [talk about what will be provided there, what you'll take advantage of, and how that will help you accomplish your goals].

- My pediatrician, Dr. Roland, always made me feel like the one from whom it was important to get information. Although he certainly asked my mother for her observations, he always turned to me and asked, "Robert, is that the way you see it?" As I grew older and understood more about medical training, I realized that Dr. Roland's ability to create a rapport with me as his patient is a result of studying at the University of Maryland School of Medicine and having been a member of a community that is person-centered and believes in the dignity of all individuals, no matter what their age. I believe I will benefit by attending the University of Maryland because, like Dr. Roland, I want to become a pediatrician, and I believe what I study as an undergraduate is an important part of my training.

Begin an essay with a quote from a book written by one of the school's professors. Continue with phrases about how studying with that professor will be meaningful to you:

- "At this stage in the writing process, the draft becomes nothing more than a fruitful scavenging ground," writes Western Washington State professor Brenda Miller in *Tell It Slant: Writing and Shaping Creative Nonfiction*. I have been writing all through high school and enjoy revising. I look forward to studying with Dr. Miller to learn how she successfully scavenges from drafts and creates publishable writing.

Finally, you might think of yourself already at the school: When I imagine myself in [name of the professor's] lectures and labs, I _____.

- When I imagine sitting in Dr. Miller's creative nonfiction writing workshop, I imagine listening to others commenting on my writing and feeling, since I've read her book *Tell It Slant: Writing and Shaping Creative Nonfiction*, that if I don't understand the responses, I can ask Dr. Miller to help me put my peers' comments to good use.

Writing the Thesis Statement for the Topic of Your Choice Option

Each of the phrases below sum up the work you will have to do in crafting your essay on the impact of special needs or circumstances on your performance, test scores not being indicative of abilities, unorthodox experience having prepared you for college, or reasons for applying to a particular school:

- My special needs have affected my studies, and my grades do not reflect my actual abilities. I have, however, learned from overcoming the obstacles these needs created, and I will bring my maturity, perseverance, and enhanced skills to my incoming class.

- I know that my test scores [or grades] do not truly reflect my academic ability because I have performed well in areas outside of class that require good quantitative and qualitative skills.

- My recent experience is unusual for a college applicant, but I believe it has fostered my abilities and will make me a valuable addition to the incoming class.

- I am applying to [name of school] because I will benefit from the program's philosophy, location, professors, activities, and talented, diverse student body.

Now you've considered the questions you might answer and made healthy starts at developing drafts that include vivid details and a shape to help you build toward insights that reflect your self-growth. Next we look at phrases to help you write the short answer for the Common Application, some of the non-Common Application essays, and the supplemental essays that schools may require in addition to the Common Application essays.

Chapter 9

A Quick Look at the Common Application Short Answer Question

Common Application Short Answer: Please briefly elaborate on one of your activities (extracurricular, personal activities, or work experience).

This is your 150-word chance to let the admissions committee know about an aspect of you that didn't get big enough play in the essay you wrote or has added more to your life than you were able to include in the essay.

Your first choice would be to use this question to tell the committee about more of your activities by writing about something that you didn't write about in the essay. If your longer essay is about an outside-of-school experience, you might want to use this one to write about a school extracurricular activity. If you wrote about a school activity in your essay, you might use this one to write about community service. If you think your application shows the academic side of you and you want to show more of the people side, you might write about an activity in which you worked with people and your community in a nonacademic way.

If you haven't discussed your love of learning, you could write about an experience that was an extension of academics, such as joining a teen book group at your local library or your church. If you haven't shown yourself to be involved in physical activities that help you balance your life, here's your chance to include one of those activities. Perhaps you've studied the martial arts or yoga outside of school and want to show how what you've learned through those disciplines has helped you cope with the stress of trying to excel in school.

Alternatively, if one activity has been central to your life and there is more to say about it to tie your involvement to more strengths and personal development, then you can use this short answer to do that. For instance, if you are an actor, musician, dancer, or athlete, you can write about an activity within that area that allowed you to use your talent to contribute to social causes, make friends, or share your skills in a meaningful way with others. If you're an elected student government official, you could write about what having the responsibility of leadership has meant to you, using specifics to show your situation, what you did, the impact, and what you learned.

The following examples show you alternative ways to start off your response to the short answer activities question.

Perfect Phrases to Help You Assess Your Activities

Have you held a meaningful job? What made it meaningful? What skills did it help you develop or see in yourself?

- I grew from the experience of working with preschoolers in an after-school program as I learned how to motivate others to learn.
- When I signed up to bag groceries at the local market, I had no idea that I would receive daily lessons in extending kindness and receiving it.

Have you done meaningful volunteer work? What has made it meaningful? What skills did it help you develop or see in yourself?

- I believe that volunteering at my local hospital has been important in developing my commitment to becoming a doctor. I learned I had the ability to communicate well with staff and patients, and I was very interested in the scientific basis of treatment.
- Volunteering as a youth counselor at my church taught me to feel comfortable with people I hardly know. It also taught me that most of us experience the same feelings and problems and need encouragement to overcome obstacles.

Have you taken on an important role in your family or with your friends or in your school? Why did you take it on? How did you feel about this, and what skills did it bring out in you? What turned out to be meaningful to you? (This role might be translator, caregiver, wage earner, negotiator, or advice-giver, among others.)

- Because my parents speak little English, I am often called on to negotiate prices for home repairs, make doctors' appointments and take my parents to them, and deal with legal paperwork. I used to be overwhelmed by the information I needed to understand, but now I am grateful for the way my situation helped me become confident and skillful.

- In any crowd, I seem to be the one who organizes fun events. I like to be among a group of people all enjoying the same adventure. I don't have trouble making arrangements, coordinating calendars, and exciting others to join me in my ideas. I have organized ski trips, trips to the beach, museum tours, and picnics. I have learned that others enjoy depending on me to brighten their social time.

What extracurricular activities have you participated in? Even if you've been participating for only a short time, what caught your interest? How have you excelled or learned new skills or made a difference through the activity? Will you continue your involvement while in college? Why and how?

- Although I have been a storyteller in the children's section of the library only since this fall, I have met with groups of children and their parents every Saturday. I have put my acting training to good use in bringing the stories alive, and I enjoyed performing in this way before an audience. I hope to find a similar program to volunteer for once I am in college.

- I joined my town's gardening club this summer and developed a passion for raising dahlias. I have learned some botany and biology as a result of my interest, and I have experienced the way bouquets of fresh flowers improve people's moods. Raising dahlias has taught me patience, soil chemistry, and how to do physical labor.

Have you won any honors, awards, or community or family recognition for one of your activities or responsibilities? What was it? How did it matter to you?

- I received a Volunteer of the Month award from the organization for the developmentally disabled where I serve dinner three times a week. The award was a gift certificate for two to the Olive Garden restaurant. I enjoyed taking my mother out to eat after we shopped one Saturday. I was touched to be appreciated, and I was touched to be able to show my appreciation to my mother who has taught me how to be kind and useful.

- I was selected to speak on behalf of my junior class on a panel that included our state representative. Students believed that I had the speech-writing ability to make their concerns clear and the manner that would ensure that their concerns would be heard by those in power. At first I was overwhelmed by the responsibility of representing so many people, but then I realized that I needed to be myself since it was being me that had won me the honor in the first place.

Have you traveled internationally? How has that contributed to your outlook and goals?

- Traveling to Europe with my parents and experiencing cities centuries older than any in the United States has changed the way I view progress. I am not sure that destroying the old in favor of the new is without drawbacks.

- Being an exchange student to Japan taught me what it is like to be an outsider and how to break down communication barriers.

Have you made use of academic programs and opportunities? Which ones? How has your participation helped you or opened up new vistas?

- Over the summer I enrolled in a community college course to brush up on my math skills. I learned the subject matter, which is helping me now, but most importantly, I learned how to handle a college class.
- I am enrolled in after-school religious training several days a week. Through this program, I have learned Hebrew, history, and theology, and I understand a lot more about world geography.

Have you created a club, organization, or chapter in your community? Why did you have to start one yourself? How has your effort paid off?

- I live in a small rural community where kids believe that not much is going on for them. Last year, I organized a school club to hold a competition for the best new idea for youth activities in our town. I enlisted support from local businesses to help us fund the winner.
- My school just added Japanese to the curriculum. When the Japanese teacher asked if some of us would like to start a Japanese club, I jumped at the chance. I have since

led in organizing a petition to our mayor about forming a sister city association with a town in the north of Japan.

Have you done your own research or self-study course in a subject you are interested in? What was it, what did you learn, and how did you go about learning it?

- When my mother was diagnosed with diabetes, I was worried every time she put anything with sugar in her mouth. I knew I didn't understand what she needed to do, and I wanted to understand thoroughly. I taught myself about the illness and effective ways to live with it by reading everything my mother brought home from the doctor's office. Then I went online and joined a Web site for family members of those with diabetes.

- I am interested in insects, and I have been studying them for years. I visit several online sites each month to read articles by internationally known entomologists, and I visit a university library near my home each month to read publications in the field. I have attended public lectures and even visited professors during their office hours.

Have you done research for something you are involved in—science club, student government, yearbook, a school play, or the school newspaper, for instance? What did you learn? What was the hardest part of the research job, and how did you overcome that to learn what you did?

- Our school science club decided to work on generating electricity. We wanted to see if we might set up solar panels for our school, as well as some windmills, and to supplement the power received from our public utility. My job was to interview city officials, university scientists, and a contractor and write up what I learned. I didn't tape the conversations, and sometimes I got wrapped up in what they were saying and forgot to write things down. It was a little awkward, but I called each one and asked more questions.

- As the head of the yearbook committee, I learned that delegating responsibilities early and checking in with committee members is crucial. The hardest part of my job was keeping track of the tasks and deadlines. I found that sometimes things fell through the cracks because of wrong assumptions. To remedy this, I learned how to make spreadsheets and use them to better track information.

Perfect Phrases for Opening the 150-Word Essay

- **As [name of role or position], I learned [short list of skills or succinct description of a lesson] by _____.**
  - As a member of the golf team, I learned concentration and focus by attending practices and meets.
  - As a teacher's assistant for second graders, I learned how much individual attention means to children.

- **When I joined [name of group or activity], I had no idea that I would [name the result or impact on you or the community].**
  - When I joined the pep rally club, I had no idea that I would end up performing for hospitalized children.
  - When I joined the prom committee, I had no idea that I would end up wanting to become a career event coordinator.

- **I am pleased that I had the opportunity to become involved in [name the activity including any positions you held] because [state lessons learned].**
  - I am pleased that I had the opportunity to become captain of the gymnastics team because I have learned how to motivate others and diffuse tension—two important leadership qualities.
  - I am pleased that I had the opportunity to sing for children in the hospital over the holidays because being a part of helping them enjoy the season made me treasure what Christmas is all about.

■ **As a first-generation U.S. citizen, I help my family and neighbors by [state activity]. Although this often means I am not able to be active with my school social group, it also means [state value to you].**
  - As a first-generation U.S. citizen, I help my family and neighbors by translating at the local free medical clinic. This means I am sometimes not able to be active with my friends after school and on some weekends. However, I'm pleased to be giving back to people who have sacrificed like my own parents so their children will have a better life.
  - As a first-generation U.S. citizen, I have helped several of my Korean neighbors negotiate legal problems by accompanying them to appointments with lawyers. This often means that I have learned private details, and I have had to become trustworthy.

■ **This year I won [or was named] _____. I learned [discuss the impact on you of the award].**
  - This year, I won first place in track and field. I learned that every winner is winning on behalf of a team.
  - This year I was named "Student of the Year" by our local newspaper. I learned that being in the limelight brings a new set of responsibilities as a role model.

■ **When I delved into [name of subject], I was surprised to learn . . .**
  - When I delved into the study of spiders, I was surprised to learn that we are almost always within four feet of one.
  - When I delved into creative writing, I was surprised to learn about a genre called creative nonfiction.

Perfect Phrases for Continuing the 150-Word Essay

- **This is how I did it:**
  - This is how I organized my research on diabetes.
  - This is how I began to master important study skills.
  - This is how I diffused the tension among my teammates.

Or:

- **Succeeding required ...**
  - Succeeding required breaking down my task into steps.
  - Succeeding required that I remain impartial and facilitate discussion among the team members.
  - Succeeding required that I call each team member once a week.

Or:

- **Because of my activities [or involvement], I [a statement of how you are different, what you know how to do, or what you believe].**
  - Because of my activities, I am a more organized person and can get almost any project done by the deadline.
  - Because of my involvement, I have developed mutual trust with my mother.
  - Because of my involvement, I no longer believe that being diagnosed with a difficult illness is the end of all one can enjoy in life.

- **I met people who taught me ...**
  - I met people who taught me how inspiring every day can be.

> – I met people who taught me that thinking about follow-through was as important as thinking about contact.
> – I met people who taught me how to track down a good school for entomology.

Your short answer essay has a tight word limit, but remember that putting in details to support your assertions is still necessary. It's the details that allow the admissions counselors to see how you've let your experience lead you to become a thoughtful, skilled person.

Chapter 10

Answering Non–Common Application Essay Questions and Supplemental Short Answer Questions

In addition to schools that don't use the Common Application and have their own essay questions, many undergraduate programs that accept the Common Application also often want essay answers to additional questions. The admissions committee will evaluate these answers, along with the Common Application essay and short answer activities question, giving you an additional opportunity to let members of the committee know about your intellectual and personal interests.

It's important to apply the same time and attention you did in writing the main essay when you write the supplemental essays. You want to give the admissions committee a good look at your writing skills and no reason to think they are variable— or worse, that you didn't write all the essays yourself.

The questions you'll come across will range from the specific to as open as the "topic of your choice" questions. Let's use Duke University for an example. In addition to the Common

Answering Non-Common Application Essay Questions

Application essay and short answer questions, Duke has its own form of the "why this school" question and two other questions. The first is, "If you have participated in any significant research activity outside of school, please provide a brief description and limit this response to one or two paragraphs." This question is similar to the short answer activities question on the Common Application. If you have participated in significant research, you would thus save it for this question and discuss a different activity in the Common Application short answer.

If you knew you were applying to Duke and lacked significant research experience, you might consider enrolling in a program that would provide you with such experience so you could write about what you learn. You could help someone in a lab or create your own project and select a teacher as a mentor to whom you'll report and with whom you'll discuss your research. You could volunteer to research a particular area for a club or organization and write a report that would be useful to the group. If your family owns a business, you could take on a research project on a topic of importance to the business.

Outside of business, you could research a topic the family needs to know more about—money management, financing a college education, a health issue, or community support services. Perhaps you can publish your findings in the school newspaper or the community newspaper. You might clerk for a law firm or a local government agency where you could take on a research project.

It's important to remember that, even if you haven't to date oriented yourself in exactly the way the school you are applying to wants, when you're in the application process, you can begin to do that by finding a suitable engagement.

Perfect Phrases for Writing about a Recent Experience to Illustrate That You Are a School's Kind of Candidate

- Although I have been involved in [name of project] only since [give a date], I have already [something you designed into the project] and learned [something you realize will be necessary for succeeding in what you've committed to do].
  - Although I have been involved in after-school tutoring only since September, I have made contributions not only by tutoring students every week, but by recruiting more tutors for our program. I have learned that sharing the load allows me to offer each of our tutees additional help building study skills.
  - Although I have been involved with the school newspaper only since September, I have already written four feature articles that ran on our front page. I also learned how to meet deadlines and work with editors.

- Now that I have begun [name of activity and for what organization], I see how important [some aspect of research] is for obtaining [name a quality about the result you want].
  - Now that I have begun attending regular meetings of our senior prom committee, I see how important doing early research into possible venues and bands will be for creating an event we will all enjoy at a cost we can afford.
  - Now that I have begun teaching grade school kids in an

after-school program, I see how important researching noncompetitive games will be for me to succeed in keeping the kids occupied and helping them form a close-knit group.

■ **Becoming involved in a research project at the beginning of my senior year has meant that I'm able to use a lot of what I've learned in [name subject or an extracurricular activity]. It has been exciting to see what happens when I apply my knowledge in a new way to [name the project].**

– Becoming involved in a research project at the beginning of my senior year has meant that I am able to use a lot of what I've learned in my science classes and as a member of our school's science club. It has been exciting to see what happens when I apply my knowledge in a new way to help people stop smoking.

– Becoming involved in a research project at the beginning of my senior year has meant that I am able to use a lot of what I've learned as a member of the orchestra for three years. It has been exciting to see what happens when I apply my knowledge of music in a new way to understand East Indian drumming.

More Types of Supplemental Questions

For another example of a school's supplemental essay questions, let's take Yale University, which requires a 500-word essay in its supplement to the Common Application:

> While we leave the topic of your second essay entirely up to you, we encourage you to use this opportunity to tell us something that we could not learn from the rest of your application. Try to pick a topic that will convey some aspect of your experience or outlook that you would like us to understand better.

If you were applying to Yale, you might choose two topics from the Common Application—one for writing the Common Application essay and one for a strategy to help you write for the Yale supplement.

You might also find, though, that you'd like to take something from the essay you wrote for the Common Application and focus on it in more detail in the supplemental essay. For instance, if you had written about an experience that influenced you and mentioned several impacts, you might take one of those impacts and further describe the situation and why it is meaningful to you. If you wrote about diversity, you might want to talk about another aspect of diversity—how you would plan to use your background in making professional goals in a global economy, for instance. Whatever you choose to write, you would make sure the two essays illustrate multiple aspects of your personality, goals, experiences, and ability to reflect on them.

Whatever application you are writing for, the following perfect phrases will help you think of material you have not yet shared.

Perfect Phrases for Focusing on What the Rest of Your Application Does Not Show the Admissions Committee

- **Few people know this about me:**
  - I have been living alone during the school year since I was a freshman because my parents returned to China when my father decided to start a company there.
  - I have started tap dance classes even though I don't believe I have a good sense of rhythm.
  - I dream of becoming an astronaut.

- **Having succeeded at [name of an activity or project], I realize [something important about what you learned]**
  - Having succeeded at becoming a member of my high school's dance troupe though I began studying ballet later than the others, I realize that I want to achieve through hard work and dedication because that brings great satisfaction.
  - Having succeeded at becoming a starting quarterback for my high school team, I realize that success demands leadership qualities, as well as dedication and practice. I plan to hone my leadership skills in every activity I pursue.

- **My philosophy of life is [state the philosophy]. I shaped my philosophy through [name activities], and it now shapes the way I live and the goals I set. [Tell the story of learning the philosophy and living it.]**
  - My philosophy of life is that practicing the Golden Rule brings joy and success. I shaped my philosophy as the

oldest in a family of eight children, and now it shapes the way I live and the goals I set outside of my family life.

– My philosophy of life is that for happiness and self-actualization you need the "right" food and the "right" stuff. I shaped my philosophy as an avid hiker.

■ **When I saw that my volunteer work [name an impact on people or the community or yourself], I began to think about [name a particular course of action].**

– When I saw that my volunteer work saved one family's Christmas from disaster, I began to think about forming an ongoing group for helping poor families enjoy other occasions more fully, especially birthdays.

– When I saw that my volunteer work visiting hospitalized children helped family members take some time for themselves while I was with their children, I began to think about creating a network of helpers in my church so families who needed relief when someone is hospitalized could get it by having others cook meals, babysit children, and drive them to activities.

■ **I have been interested in [name of a subject] since [something you did or saw], and so far I have learned [discuss what is important to you about the subject].**

– I have been interested in biological systems since my mother began her vegetable garden when I was 10. So far I have learned a lot about the way organisms feed off one another.

– I have been interested in nursing since my aunt took me to work with her to observe a day in the life of a maternity ward nurse. So far I have learned a lot about the opportunities for nurses in various fields and a lot about their important functions in each setting.

In some cases, you may want to use a supplemental question to address a quirk in your nature that is so much a part of your personality that others identify you by the quirk. Stanford University, newly added to the list of schools accepting the Common Application, remains committed to its 10-line application question about what you would write in a note to a future roommate to reveal something about yourself. Although an applicant could use the opportunity to brag about an accomplishment, many believe this question is meant not to elicit information about accomplishments but as an opportunity for the applicant to focus on his or her personality.

"I mean, really, would you tell your future roommate that you won Regional Soccer Championships or that you apologize in advance for being a snorer?" a student offered in an online post.

Perfect Phrases for Revealing Something Quirky about Yourself

■ **When I am engaged in [name of activity], I [name a behavior like becoming so focused you don't hear the telephone or forget to eat].**

- When I am engaged in a book, I often don't hear people talking to me.
- When I leave for a trip, I try very hard to take only the clothes I'll need so I will have room to bring back some new clothing.

■ **My outside-of-school passions include [name a hobby that you hope to continue at school and tell how you will do that].**

- My outside-of-school passions include learning how to rock climb. So far I have been reading about my passion, but when I get to college, I plan to find a rock-climbing club through the Sierra Club.
- Outside of school, I am passionate about growing orchids. When I get to college, I plan to study botany and join a horticultural club.

■ **My nickname is _____. My classmates and family call me that because _____.**

- My nickname is Quirk. My classmates and family call me that because I often do things a little bit differently from others.
- My nickname is Bug. My classmates and family call me that because I love driving my VW Beetle and belong to several online groups that trade info on the classic car.

- **My sister [or brother or best friend] told me I should [name something]. I did it by . . .**
  - My sister told me I should find out more about auditioning for a community theater since I loved to act. I did this by going to our town's arts commission office.
  - My best friend convinced me to try out for our town's a cappella chorus because she thought my voice was really good. I got my courage up by singing for her and three other friends and recording my singing.

- **If I read about a [place, food, activity, online site] new to me, I am obsessed with learning more about it. To do this, I . . .**
  - If I read about food new to me, I am obsessed with learning more about it. To do this, I begin with an online search. I read recipes using the food, the history of the food, and where to purchase or order it.
  - If I read a word that is new to me, I am obsessed with learning how to use it myself. I do this by going to the *Oxford English Dictionary* and learning the word's history and meaning. Then I write a letter to a friend describing this word and using it.

- **If I had only one day on campus, I would . . .**
  - If I had only one day on campus, I would visit the new state-of-the-art gymnasium. As an aspiring architect, I am interested in the construction of this gym and the way it houses hundreds of people playing a variety of sports.
  - If I had only one day on campus, I would visit the special edition archives at the university library. I would like to read the early chapbooks of now-famous poets.

- **Sometimes I imagine I am President [or a senator or a professor or Bill Gates or Pablo Picasso or any number of people in powerful positions or celebrated as artists]. Here is what I would most admire about myself and my actions:**
  - Sometimes I imagine I am President. Here is what I would most admire about myself and my actions: I set up a world conference on global warming to which I invite hikers and mountain climbers because they are people from across the world who have actually seen glaciers shrinking. I believe that if they show slides from their years at locations where temperatures are changing, politicians will be moved to quicker action.
  - Sometimes I imagine I am George Clooney. I am reading over many scripts to decide what I will produce and act in next. I am on the lookout for a script by a teenager because I believe there are new points of view emerging.
- **I am bringing something unusual with me to school. [Describe what and why.]**
  - I am bringing a shard from a mirror that was my grandmother's. It is the only tangible object she has from her childhood, which was spent in Auschwitz, and it inspires me to study so I can become a political leader.
  - I am bringing my antique embroidery hoop with me. My grandmother taught me to embroider the way her mother taught her, and she gave me this hoop. I find that doing the stitching relaxes and restores me after studying.

The other two Stanford short answer questions are:

- Sharing intellectual interests is an important aspect of

university life. Describe an idea or experience that you find intellectually exciting, and explain why.

■ What makes Stanford a special place for you?

We'll address the short answer about an idea you find stimulating next. The short answer about what makes Stanford special is a version of the "why this school" question. Remember, whenever you find a question like this, be sure to read the college's mission statement to understand how to be sure your answer connects with the school's mission, whether you are talking about location, student body, particular professors, the program, courses, or the fact that a relative attended.

Perfect Phrases for Describing Intellectual Interests, Ideas, or Experiences, and Why You Find Them Exciting

- **When I learned in class that [name a scientific or mathematical hypothesis], I [discuss what you found meaningful and intriguing].**
  - When I learned in class that honey might be useful in curing illnesses, I started thinking about majoring in chemistry and ultimately understanding common natural substances and their medicinal and cleaning uses for humans.
  - When I learned in class that an AIDS vaccine had failed in trials and disappointed many, I realized I wanted to become a bench scientist and help pharmaceutical companies get cures out into the world safely and quickly.

- **When I attended a lecture by [name an intellectual], I heard [state the idea or construction put forth], and I realized [discuss the impact of what you'd heard].**
  - When I attended a lecture by Professor Z, I heard him relate that using corn oil fuel wasn't actually going to help us reduce car emissions. I realized that just because something is grown rather than pumped out of the earth, it isn't the be-all end-all solution. I look forward to learning research and analytical skills.
  - When I attended a lecture by Nancy Pearl, a famous librarian who worked for the Washington Center for the Book, she told the audience about scores of authors on a variety of subjects. I realized that librarians store a vast

amount of knowledge, and I decided to investigate becoming one.

- **When I read [name a book or magazine article] and came across [quote or paraphrase an idea], I began thinking [discuss the implications of the idea that excite you].**
    - When I read *Forever Lily* by Beth Nonte Russell and came across writing that includes descriptions of the author's dreams juxtaposed with daily events during a trip to China, I realized I had a story to write that way.
    - When I read *Writing to Change the World* by Mary Pipher, I came across this quote from Oliver Wendell Holmes: "The mind, once expanded to the dimensions of bigger ideas, never returns to its original size." I began thinking about the injustice in the way my father's family chided him about going to college, accusing him, the only one of the group who got a degree, of having "big ideas."

- **Synthesizing thoughts and ideas is my passion. Recently, I came across the information that [name an idea or fact] and the [name another idea or fact]. I realized that together these two pieces of information mean that [talk about a synthesis of the two that you made].**
    - Synthesizing thoughts and ideas is my passion. I came across information recently about a syndrome in which hostages become loyal to those who control them. I also read that when given power over others, people very easily use it harmfully. I began to wonder if the hostage who supported a tormentor wasn't gaining something psychologically by imagining himself in power. When I take psychology classes, I intend to investigate this hypothesis.

– Synthesizing thoughts and ideas is my passion. I recently learned that mixing herbs and flowers in the same garden bed is stylish now. Working part-time at the Gap, I have also been thinking about the way merchants are taught that people like a certain amount of clutter around them when they shop so they can have fun "weeding" their way through the merchandise. Putting these two thoughts together, I have begun visualizing my own shop, where children's and adult's toys are artfully mixed with clothing for the whole family.

Some schools are very elaborate in the way they set up their short answer questions. Studying what Tufts wants in its 50-word short answer answer, two 220-word short essays, and one optional essay on any of seven topics will help you develop strong ideas for approaching many college application essays. The following is from Tufts 2007 application:

I. REQUIRED SHORT ANSWER (50 words)

"Education does not accomplish anything if it does not stretch your mind, if it does not force you to think about things in new ways, if it does not challenge you to examine some of your assumptions," writes Provost Jamshed Bharucha. Describe the aspects of Tufts' curriculum or undergraduate program that prompted your application.

This is, of course, the "why this particular school" essay, but with a special spin. For this version of the essay, candidates must focus on something in the Tufts curriculum or undergraduate program that promises to help them think in new ways. The inclusion of the provost's mission statement in the question demands this from the candidates. Your job is to show how that attracted you to applying to Tufts is about stretching and thinking in new ways.

Perfect Phrases for Writing about Stretching and Thinking in New Ways

■ Just thinking about participating in [name a particular course, text, club, event, or program at the school you are applying to], I begin to question assumptions I've been taught. [Pose one or more as questions: Is the United States a true democracy? What motivates an atheist toward moral behavior? Can working in groups of diverse people enhance communication? After posing the question, write a short description of how the particular program, course, or club will help you explore new ways of understanding and acting.]

– Just thinking about participating in the college drama club, I am beginning to question assumptions about my being too shy to stand in front of others. Could I really gather the courage to do this? Because the club is described as having a troupe approach to performance, I believe I will not only be able to entertain others but benefit from being part of a group.

– Just thinking about going to a school with an urban campus, I am beginning to question the idea that universities are ivory towers, sealed off so scholars can think without being distracted. Is it really better to be further away from the action? From the course catalog, I see that classes use the city's many programs and departments as a kind of laboratory that allows research to become relevant and have immediate impact.

■ I read about [name of activity, course, program, professor] and realized that by participating, I could investigate my own beliefs about [name a topic]. I want to appreciate more than I have been able to from the assumptions my community makes and insists are true: [name the assumptions and briefly discuss how you will make your own investigation to learn more about the subject].

– I read about Professor J holding weekly seminars open to the community on negotiating health care, and I realized that by participating, I could investigate issues that exist in health-care delivery and better prepare myself for medical studies.

– I read about the "Learning to Become an 18C Sailor" course and realized that by participating, I would learn geography, history, first aid, physics, and boat craft.

- **When I was visiting the campus, I saw students [name what they were doing—like studying in groups or meeting informally with a professor or being respectful of the professor's position and knowledge]. I realized [name your realization and tell how having it matters to you].**

– When I was visiting the campus, I saw students from many ethnic backgrounds gathered in the student union studying together. I realized that college is a place where I will benefit from the experience of peers, as well as from coursework.

– When I was visiting the campus, I saw professors meeting in one-on-one sessions with students, and I realized that this school takes a personal interest in students' progress.

- ■ I want to gain [name a trait that involves stretching yourself] from my college education. [Name of school] promises to help me meet my goal with [its selection of courses, specific courses, location, extracurricular program, volunteer activities]. Here's how I imagine myself growing:
  - – I want to gain a background in political science from my college education. Georgetown promises to help me meet my goal, not only with its many courses taught by professors involved in policy making, but with its array of internships.
  - – I want to gain a background in finance from my college education. Columbia University promises to help me meet my goal with Wall Street internships and investment clubs.

Tufts second short answers are longer:

II. REQUIRED SHORT ESSAYS (200 words each)

1. Describe the environment in which you were raised— your family, home, neighborhood or community—and how it influenced the person you are today.

This question can be tackled just like the Common Application number 1 or number 3 question: the significant experience evaluation or the person who influenced your essay.

2. Self-identity and personal expression take many forms. Music, food, art, and clothing can make a statement. Politics, religion, nationality, and ethnicity often act as defining attributes. Colored wristbands and blogs

express opinions and viewpoints while the minutiae that adorn a refrigerator or a notebook can be clues to someone's passions. Are you an oldest child? Do you surf? Are you a vegetarian? Did you wear flip-flops to the prom? Do you have a tattoo? Who are you?

Answering this one can be like answering the topic of your choice question where you discuss an unconventional experience that affected how you behave, what you believe, and what inspires you. However, for Tufts, the way in is with a personal description of quirks—you might get to the diversity experience by describing a tattoo or a bracelet or a hairstyle that identifies you or would fool someone about your background. Moreover, this question wants you to address passion, what is uniquely you, whatever else is true about your background and skills. You can use the perfect phrase discussed under Stanford's what-would-you-write-your-future-roommate-about-yourself question. Whatever physical trait or birth order you relate, make sure you connect it to what you honor, love, or can't get enough of.

Perfect Phrases for Showing Who You Are in a Vivid Manner

- **I wear [name something characteristic of you that you believe makes a statement] every day [or to special events] because . . .**
  - I wear Crocs every day, even to weddings, because I like the bright colors and comfort.
  - I wear a suit and tie to school one day out of every week. I believe that dressing in this way makes a good impression on my teachers.

- **The music that I listen to [or play] is [name the music]. Its impact [reminds me, moves me, focuses my attention on] . . .**
  - The music that I listen to is usually by Mozart. Its impact is to remind me of something larger than my day's problems and irritations.
  - I listen to the Beatles. I like the stories their songs tell, and since they were writing their music 40 years ago, I realize that my parents and grandparents had concerns similar to the ones I have.

- **I make [name food] just the way my mother and her mother before her did. [Tell what the process and the food mean to you.]**
  - I make a coconut cake for people's birthdays just the way my mother and her mother before her did. We are from Haiti, and each ingredient reminds me of our family stories.
  - In the winter, I make stuffed cabbage with raisins just as

my mother and grandmother did. The sweet and sour ingredients simmer and make me think about our family history and triumphs despite setbacks and sadness.

- **The art I hang in my room is [name it]. I like it around me because ...**
  - I have posters of France on all four walls of my room. I like being surrounded by pictures of the Eiffel Tower and sidewalk cafés because I am learning French and plan to enroll in the college's junior year abroad program.
  - I have prints by water colorist Diana Madaras in my room. Her renditions of the Tucson desert inspire me to paint and to put my vision into an environment others may feel is bland.

- **I'm pretty sure that my passion for [name activity] has made all the difference in the way I [view something, have skill in certain areas, or have found life satisfying].**
  - I'm pretty sure that my passion for ballet has made all the difference in the way I have found my high school career satisfying. When I was selected to dance the lead in this year's Nutcracker, I knew hard work and dedication would pay off.
  - I'm pretty sure that my passion for football has made all the difference in helping me learn to mentor others.

- **As the [youngest, oldest, middle] child of [number of kids in the family], I have developed the following traits:**
  - As the oldest of three children, I have developed a sense of responsibility as well as the ability to help others while meeting my own needs.

- As the youngest of seven children, I have learned gratitude for having so much help in life.

■ **As an adopted child, I am particularly sensitive to [name a way of looking at or wondering about the world].**

- As an adopted child, particularly sensitive to differences between my adoptive family and myself, I am always interested in scientific studies about nature and nurture.

- As an adopted child, I feel a particular sense of obligation to my parents who nurtured me.

■ **Since my grandparents raised me, I [name a way of looking at or wondering about the world or a trait of yours].**

- Since my grandparents raised me on a farm, I know a lot about living life by seasons and organizing household chores that way.

- Since my grandparents raised me, I had stricter rules than most of my friends, but I felt nurtured by the rules rather than bothered by them.

■ **As a child of divorce, I [name a way of looking at relationships and the world or a trait of yours].**

- As a child of divorce, I seek long-term relationships and work hard to sustain the ones I have.

- As a child of divorce, I understand that relationships can successfully transform into new ones.

■ **As the child of a single parent, I [name a way of looking at the world or relationships or name a trait of yours].**

- As the child of a single parent, I developed a sense of responsibility quite early.

- As the child of a single parent, I got a close-up view of how to successfully multitask.

Answering Non–Common Application Essay Questions

- **As a child in a blended family, [name a trait of yours, or a way of looking at or relating to people or seeing the world].**
  - As a child in a blended family, I learned how to overcome jealousy and shyness to build strong relationships.
  - As a child in a blended family, I learned that differences in how we celebrate holidays can add pleasure rather than detract from it.

- **As the only [name ethnic group] in my church [or class or neighborhood], I have learned to [name a way of looking at or wondering about the world or people].**
  - As the only person of Egyptian origin in my class, I have learned how to join in activities new to me and invite others to share in activities new to them.
  - As the only Jewish student in my class, I have learned how to share my heritage and educate others about some of the background of their own religions.

- **Because my parents haven't taught me as much as I'd like about the culture they are from, I have [name activities and classes you have taken to reconnect with your heritage].**
  - Because my parents haven't passed on as much about the culture they are from as I would like, I have enrolled in Hebrew classes.
  - Because my parents haven't taught me as much about the culture they are from as I want to know, I have begun to study Mao and the Chinese revolution.

The Tufts application sets up its optional essay this way:

> Tufts is dedicated to developing leaders who will address the intellectual and social challenges of the new century. Critical thinking, creativity, practicality and wisdom are four elements of successful leadership, and the following topics offer you an opportunity to illustrate the various elements of your leadership skills. We invite you to choose one of the optional essays found below and prepare an essay of 250–400 words.

Next, the application provides seven questions to choose from:

1. The late scholar James O. Freedman referred to libraries as "essential harbors on the voyage toward understanding ourselves." What work of fiction or non-fiction would you include in a personal library? Why?

You probably recognize this as a variation of Common Application question 4. This time, though, you might discuss not only the way the work has influenced you, but also how it will prove valuable as you continue to grow and learn, the reason you would keep it in your library.

2. An American adage states "curiosity killed the cat." If that is correct, why do we celebrate people like Galileo, Lincoln, and Gandhi, individuals who thought about longstanding problems in new ways or who defied conventional thinking to achieve great results?

As fulfilling curiosity leads to significant experience, you could answer this one with a slight variation of question 1 of the Common Application question by describing an event that illustrates how a risk you took to fulfill your curiosity positively affected you or others. You would then discuss how the outcome disproves the adage. You would also show how the impact of an event or risk you took was positive and how it illustrates why you celebrate those who think in new ways.

Alternatively, using a variation of Common Application question 2, you could discuss your new way of thinking about a personal, local, national, or international concern and how this led to results that prove that fulfilling curiosity nurtures the intellect and society.

A smart thing to do, of course, would be to look up what Galileo, Lincoln, and Gandhi thought about in new ways and how the world received their thoughts. You might discuss what in their experience motivates you.

3. History's great events often turn on small moments. For example, what if Rosa Parks had given up her seat on that Montgomery bus in 1955? What if Pope John Paul I had not died in 1978 after a month in office? What if Gore had beaten Bush in Florida and won the 2000 U.S. presidential election? Using your knowledge of American or world history, choose a defining moment and imagine an alternative historical scenario if that key event had played out differently.

You can envision this essay as an "historical figure who had an influence on you" answer (Common Application question number 5) in reverse—you get to decide what would have happened if one of these people's lives had gone differently. To write an answer, think about those peo-ple's influence over events in history that have affected your life (as you would for Common Application question 5) and then think of what would have happened if they could have done more or had not done what they had.

Although you might not be a history buff, you might find it interesting to answer this kind of question if you allowed yourself to think closer to home. It is difficult, maybe impossible, to predict what other social forces might have come or not come into play should one thing in his-tory not have happened. There is always action and reac-tion, and history is full of surprises. So, the closer to home the defining moment you select to work with, the more detailed your answer will be and the more it will convey information about you.

Perfect Phrases for Thinking about Things Going Differently

■ If [person who influenced you] hadn't [name of an action or involvement in some historical moment that defined this person's life], my life may have turned out very differently. [Write a description of your world as it might have been; name the valuable aspects of your life that you would not have experienced. Discuss the ways you value what you have learned or accomplished because of the way things did turn out.]

  – If Rosa Parks hadn't decided that she was too tired to stand at the back of the bus, my life would have turned out very differently. As an African-American student from the South, I might not have gone to schools that were well funded and had good college preparation.

  – If President Clinton had not disappointed the American people with inappropriate sexual behavior, I believe Democrats would have kept their power in the White House, and we would not be involved in a war with Iraq. Today, we could be spending billions more on research and education and controlling carbon emissions.

■ If [name a legislator who introduced a bill or a contemporary writer who wrote an influential book or investigative article or a student movement that brought world attention to a country or a world leader who addressed the United Nations] hadn't let the world know about [name an issue], the [name a result] we [in a particular state, country, or part of the world] enjoy today might not be available.

- If Al Gore had not made his now famous movie, *An Inconvenient Truth*, and helped Americans know the evidence for and impact of global warming, the rapid increase in manufacturing electric cars for the U.S. market might not have occurred.
- If new lawyers Sarah Weddington and Linda Coffee had not challenged the constitutionality of Texas law on abortion in 1972 because they wanted to establish a new constitutional right allowing women to control their own bodies, I believe women's success in corporate and religious America would not have happened quickly.

Or:

■ **If you want to take on a hypothesis that shows your political leanings, you might imagine a redistribution of government funds and emphasis and write a thesis statement making your point:**

- If our country had spent the billions it has spent on the war in Iraq on developing our educational system's knowledge of Middle Eastern history, religion, politics, art, and political thinking, many agencies and individuals may have succeeded in building stronger, more democratic populations through trade and cultural exchanges, despite repressive governments. [You would go on to show how people, business, and the arts have influenced many cultures over the years.]
- If Colin Powell had remained in charge of the armed forces, I believe generals would have had more say in

logistics and tactics, and outcomes would have included a shorter war and a stronger Iraq today. [You would go on to show how his thinking and policies would have made the difference and had the impact you describe.]

Perfect Phrases for Understanding Short Story Basics

Here's question 4 from the Tufts list asking you to write a short story:

4. Create a short story using one of the following topics:
   The end of MTV
   Confessions of a Middle School Bully
   The Professor Disappeared
   The Mysterious Lab

A short story is a different piece of writing from an essay. It has a protagonist, an antagonist (person or situation that makes for conflict), plot, characters, setting, voice, and point of view. People read the fiction of authors they admire and learn much about the art of fiction writing from their reading. If you tackle a question like this, reread stories you have enjoyed, as well as material on short story writing. One enjoyable book on the craft is Josip Novakovich's *Fiction Writer's Workshop* from Writer's Digest Books.

Here are some of the basics for doing this type of essay:

A persona's voice: It can be the voice of an unreliable narrator, like the character short story writer Ron Carlson created who, on seeing that his wife had cleared out, believed Bigfoot stole her. It can be in the voice of an improbable narrator like Bigfoot himself in another of Carlson's stories. Success can come using a narrator based on someone in your environment you would like to understand better. You might make up a life situation that has caused the shyness of the shyest girl in the class. Or you might create a story about a class jock who keeps his interest in gardening a secret.

Obstacles: Short story protagonists, the personas we identify with as readers, the ones the story is about, must face obstacles—these can come from outside of themselves or from traits within. Always, the main character wants or requires something but someone or some situation keeps him or her from getting it. The story is the way the protagonist is blocked and what the protagonist does to achieve what he or she needs, with or without success.

Plot: This involves the order in which the protagonist faces obstacles, who or what presents the obstacles and how, and the success and lack of success the protagonist has in overcoming them. There is the setup—who the story is about, where the story takes place, what is going on just as the story opens. Then something happens to spin the plot in a new direction. As the protagonist works to get needs met, something else happens that yet again spins the story in a new direction, presenting new obstacles or situations. These can be subtle. They don't involve huge outer events. The ringing of a phone when the speaker has given up on receiving an important call or pages of an important assignment blowing away in the wind can prove significant. Ultimately, something happens that allows the protagonist to achieve some sort of inner satisfaction or resolution even if the original need isn't met in the way he or she had hoped.

Setting: When readers can fully imagine where a story takes place, they are happier readers. When an author puts details of place on the page, the story's characters have more to relate to and thus can show more of themselves. Dress a scene, as a stage is dressed. Relate the time of day through the lighting. Describe the objects in the room to help the reader understand the environment the characters are in, and include the sounds, smells, and tastes the characters are experiencing. You might write more than you need and then trim down the text to the words that best evoke the mood and situation you are writing about. But by putting in sensory information, you will make the situation more real to yourself, and thus have more to work with as you write.

Point of view: Who tells the story determines the details and the mood and tone. A story is told well when we believe that the person telling it could have known what he or she is telling and speaks in language we believe he or she would use.

If the person telling the story goes to the basement for something and while she is down there, another character upstairs considers whether to open the door, switching points of view as follows doesn't work:

- Gilda knew that her birthday party was going to be a success. She wanted to make sure she made the best decorations anyone had ever seen. So she went downstairs to check in the supply cabinet her father kept in the basement. As she peered inside the cabinet, she heard the muffled sound of a knock on the front door. Meanwhile, Alice was sitting on the couch upstairs. She didn't know whether the person at the door might be a stranger. She couldn't decide if she should open the door.

The main narrator can only know what is possible from

where she is: "When Gilda heard the muffled sound of a knock at the front door, she considered how Alice must be wondering if she should open the door."

Tone: If the person telling the story goes in and out of sounding consistently like himself or herself, readers lose interest. Someone who is describing a situation with big words has to be someone readers believe has a reason for knowing so many big words. Someone who is eight years old, unless presented as extraordinary, is not going to suddenly exclaim, "Well, I was amazed to see the bifurcated stem of the plant."

Perfect Phrases for Discussing Risk

The fifth question on the Tufts list deals with issues involving risk-taking.

5. Describe a moment in which you took a risk and achieved an unexpected goal. How did you persuade others to follow your lead? What lessons do you draw from this experience? You may reflect on examples from your academic, extracurricular, or athletic experiences.

This question works like Common Application question number 1. In answering this question, you would choose an experience where (1) you stood up for something to enlist others in helping you achieve an important goal, (2) tested yourself against someone or something to gain support, or (3) experienced failure and/or ridicule before people saw the correctness of what you were asking or doing.

Using phrases like the ones that follow will help you spin the question so you best use your personal experience.

■ **No one else seemed ready to speak up, so I raised my hand. [Quote what you said on a controversial topic concerning your classmates, a program, or a community issue.] There was no going back as [discuss what happened, what you had to do, and what was gained— include questions and comments by others and what you did to help them support you].**

– No one else seemed ready to speak up, so I raised my hand. I told the teacher and the class that I believed we had to speak out at the upcoming Board of Education meeting. Our football coach was being undermined by parents angry about his decision to throw football team members off the team for attending a party where alcohol was served. They had each signed a contract that said they wouldn't do this, and it seemed unfair that the school was considering reinstating the players who were not taking responsibility for defying their agreement. There was no going back now, even though many of the kids in my class were friends of the players. I said that I was not against the students, but didn't want to see a qualified coach undermined. I felt that if the school wasn't going to uphold rules, then any of us at any time could decide to behave in a destructive manner without fear of consequences. There had to be a different way to solve this problem.

- **I wasn't going to [name an action like joining an activity, making a friend, doing something that frightened you]. Yet, on [date], I did just that. [Describe what you did; list and discuss the results/describe what you gained.]**

– I was angry about my family's move. I promised myself that I wasn't going to try to make friends in the new senior class I was forced to enter. But on October 15, 2007, I did just that. I was in the library studying until my mother came to pick me up. I noticed a boy from my science class reading a new issue of *Scientific American*. I love that magazine and told him that. It wasn't long before we were talking about the inventions we made for science competitions and how we'd both gone to state competitions with our teams. He invited me to join the school's science club.

- **When I heard these words, [quote what someone you didn't trust or admire demanded], I knew I had to [name action taken]. [Discuss why you had to do what you did.]**
  – When I overheard the words, "Let's keep our meetings a secret," I knew I had to influence my friends to be open with the rest of the school committee that was planning the Christmas program. Christmas is about connecting to one another. The thought of having two groups, at odds with one another, planning the program seemed out of line. [You would go on to discuss how you got the group to be open and the good result that came from that.]

- **When I heard these words, [quote what someone you do trust or admire related], I knew I had to [name action taken]. [Discuss why you had to do what you did.]**
  – When my mother told me that visiting our terminally ill neighbor on a regular basis would build my character, I was dubious. I knew I had to do what my mother was the suggesting or I would feel guilty, but I didn't know how a high school student could have anything meaningful to say to a 65-year-old woman who had only months to live. [You would go on to discuss how you found things in common and how your contact built your character.]

- **When I read [quote something that motivated you to an action or way of reevaluating yourself or situation], I saw something new about [state the topic]. [Discuss what you realized, what you did, and the results.]**

- When I read that animal shelters in Seattle were in deplorable condition, I decided to become a volunteer at the shelter near me. I love animals and felt that I could contribute by helping at one shelter and perhaps making conditions better there. What I found out was that facilities were incredibly overcrowded and even with many volunteers to walk and exercise the dogs, there were too many hours in a day that animals were in cramped conditions. I decided to join a task force that reported to the mayor's office. [You would go on to discuss your role in the task force and what you learned and the impact you had on the group.]

- **Others were skeptical, but I [state the project you took on]. I had to because . . . It wasn't until [state an action or event] that others joined me. Happy to have the others helping, I [show how you organized, what was accomplished, and how you know it was meaningful.]**

- My friends were skeptical, but I decided to address the litter problem at my school. I handed out fliers with a meeting date and place. Just like my friends thought, no one showed up except one person. That person was the reporter from our school newspaper. He ran an article showing me at the front of an empty meeting room. That's when others began contacting me to join in the group. Happy to have others helping me, I led in arranging cleanups and getting more trash cans stationed around the school, but what I valued learning was the impact of the media.

Perfect Phrases for Thinking about Unsatisfied Intellectual Passions and How to Use Them for the Greater Good

Question 6 on the Tufts list deals with unsatisfied intellectual passions:

6. A high school curriculum does not always afford much intellectual freedom. Describe one of your unsatisfied intellectual passions. How might you apply this interest to serve the common good and make a difference in society?

Thinking of strategies used for Common Application question number 5 but focusing on intellectual diversity will help here. The question then becomes an opportunity to show how you think for yourself, the obstacles you've faced in doing so, and for what reason (future goal) you have done so. Alternatively, you might think of something you've always wanted to do when you "grow up" and discuss its social importance.

- I have only just begun pursuing [name the intellectual pursuit]. It has been difficult doing this as a high school student because [name the reason or reasons you have felt limited]. At first, I [discuss what you did in your as-yet-unsatisfied intellectual pursuit]. Then, I encountered [name the obstacle]. To continue my pursuit, I [talk about what you did to overcome the obstacle]. Soon, I will [tell what you will do based on the lesson in overcoming the obstacle]. I believe what I learn will help me make a difference by [discuss what actions you will take in the world, what you might create with others, or what field you might enter].

- During high school, I was unable to [name an intellectual pursuit you would have pursued if you could have] because [give a reason such as funds, resources, location, time, age, legal, or social group limitations]. However, I [write about what you did do—research, learn about resources, make a plan for later]. As a college student, I will [name how you will proceed, including courses you will take, clubs you will join or create, and volunteer work and internships you'll become involved in]. I believe that my continued passion and involvement will result in [discuss what you will be able to do or set in motion and how that will address a problem people or societies face].

- As a high school student, in addition to my studies, extracurricular activities, and typical teen personal life, I have begun to explore [name area of interest you have been exploring]. I've taken on this interest now even though I can't yet make the difference I want to. [Discuss the difference you want to make and then give the reason you haven't satisfied that goal yet—the obstacles to doing this.] Even though fully acting from my knowledge is not yet possible, [say why], I have learned [discuss what you learned]. My plan for attaining a position from which I can make an impact is this . . .

Perfect Phrases for Evaluating the Design Option

Question 7 from Tufts deals with using your creativity and design talents:

7. Using an 8.5 x 11-inch sheet of paper, create an ad for a movie, design a house, make an object better, and illustrate an ad for an object.

Tired of writing essays? Feel designing something or presenting in bytes and pictures might best display your creativity? Here's your chance for schools that offer a nonliterary means of expressing yourself, including PowerPoint slides for demonstrating your design creativity. Of course, if you choose this opportunity, you are most likely a person who has thought about ads, designs, and inventions for quite a while and may already have something you have worked up that you can polish for the application. If you include text, make sure you've thoroughly proofread even the simplest sentences and phrases. Today, presentation skills and an ability to express essential ideas in key points are important in many fields and in many cross-cultural settings. Still, minimal as the language employed in those presentations may be, proper word choice, punctuation, and grammar are important.

In taking on this question, here are some points to keep in mind:

■ Can my ad or design for a house or for the improvement of an object stand alone and communicate all I want to a viewer?

- Have I checked into specs for designs before presenting mine so I am using recognized formats? Have I consulted with a graphic design professional or commercial arts teacher for references on designing criteria and presentation techniques?
- Is what I am sending neatly presented with every aspect clearly drawn?
- Are all the words I've used legible and spelled correctly?
- Have I gone the extra mile to make sure my design or ad is eye-catching?
- Is what I am sending unnecessarily cluttered with extra text or markings?
- Is every feature the eye must see large enough?

Perfect Phrases for Articulating a Major Project Idea

Recognizing More Patterns for Supplemental Essays

Looking at supplemental essay questions is a big help for learning more about how to hone your answers, whether they are for supplemental questions or for the Common Application questions. The more you learn about how to read a question so the way it's stated helps you organize your answer and the more you learn about how to put things together, the stronger and more convincing your writing will be. Like Tufts' supplemental questions, Sarah Lawrence's options are elaborately written, providing missionlike statements in the body of the three questions offered for candidates to select from, all of which tell what the school is most interested in knowing about its applicants:

The first of three options is:

A central part of learning at Sarah Lawrence is conference work, the guided independent study on a topic of the students' choosing that accompanies each seminar course. Conference work is a result of a student's specific area of interest in a class and a teacher's guidance; most often this semester- or year-long course of study culminates in a substantial paper, project, or piece of research. For this essay, we offer you the chance to imagine what you might do for conference work. Is there a topic you've always wanted to learn more about? Has a class in high school rushed past a subject that you found fascinating? The topic can be as broad or as narrow as you would like.

This question is much like Tufts' intellectual pursuit question and can be handled the same way. The impact of the intellectual pursuit for this question will be a project, paper, or body of research that is meaningful to some group or to you as a stepping-stone to a future career or activity. Here are some ways to talk about what you might do:

- I would most like to offer [name a group or field of study] original ideas and solutions [or choreography, a musical score, collection of poems, the founding of an organization, etc.]. To do this, I must [explain the tasks you see ahead]. I would like to take advantage of offerings such as [name the courses, programs, options the college offers] and work with [name of professor or organization or program at the school] to accomplish my goal.

- As a graduate of [name of school], I want to have a track record of contributing in my area of interest. Toward that end, I will [describe the project you will put together and how you will go about the work of fulfilling your goal].

- In high school, I read about [or participated in or heard a lecture on] [name of area of interest]. It wasn't long before I [or "I stowed my interest away until I could"] … At this point in my life, I am ready to [name what you can do to further your participation in the field you are describing]. [Describe specific ways you can use the programs and location of the college to help you.]

Perfect Phrases for Describing How You Have Grown and How This Particular College Will Help You Continue to Grow

The second Sarah Lawrence option is:

We assume that you have changed throughout your high school years, and we are curious to hear what experiences and challenges in the past four years have influenced who you have become. We are also interested in how these changes have led you to apply to Sarah Lawrence College. What is it about the college and its unique educational structure that leads you to think that you will be a good fit? How will the college help you fulfill your goals?

This is the influences question combined with the why-this-school question but with a mandatory spin—the reason you have chosen this school is part of how you have grown and changed in the last four years. So although you may have always wanted to attend Sarah Lawrence or any other school you are writing for, there has to be something you mention in your essay that shows you have learned what makes the school a fit for the talented, sensitive, aware, prepared college entrant you have become. If you have always wanted to attend the school, you might show how the school's idea of its student and graduates has been one of the things influencing your growth during high school.

Here are some phrases for taking on this question:

■ During high school, I have become more of the person I want to be through my participation in [name of an activity]. The participants, our leader, and my own evaluation of my performance offered me the opportunity to grow. [Describe the way each contributed to your growth.] I believe I am a good fit for [name of college] because [describe how you will take advantage of the programs, classes, activities, and location of the school to continue developing yourself in the areas you described at your essay's opening].

- Before [building a house for Habitat for Humanity, going to State in athletics or music, losing a best friend, taking a specific course], I hadn't thought about [name a spiritual or social or intellectual problem such as how teamwork offers results larger than the sum of the parts, how the death of someone close to you changes your outlook forever, how much difference one individual can make, how connected physics and mathematics are to philosophy]. Now, I see that [name specific qualities you admire in yourself and others or specific understandings you have]. [Describe how you will take advantage of the programs, classes, activities, and location of the school to continue developing yourself in the areas you described at the opening of your essay.]

- My teachers, parents, and friends have each seen a part of who I am. [Tell what each has seen.] I am beginning to understand how the parts of my personality and character all contribute to making me a person who can [name a field you want to enter or a goal you want to fulfill with your life]. At [name of college], I will be able to [name what you will participate in]. With this experience, I will be able to [describe how you will contribute to the school as an undergraduate student]. When I graduate, I will be [discuss the goals you'll be prepared to fulfill and how you will continue to be involved with your alma mater, helping future undergraduates achieve their goals].

Perfect Phrases for Describing How You Have Begun Learning Who You Are and How This Specific College Will Help You Continue to Do That

The third Sarah Lawrence option is:

> Many Sarah Lawrence alumni credit the college for helping them find their voice—whether as scientists, performers, activists, and lawyers or simply as educated individuals. Do you feel as if you have found your voice, and if so, what factors and experiences helped you do so? How do you think Sarah Lawrence and its unique educational structure will help you develop or discover your voice?

It is probably best with this one to emphasize what you know of developing a voice—how it doesn't come all at once but by trying things out, listening to what others respond to you. This helps you hear yourself more clearly, how you feel when you commit to particular projects and responsibilities, how that feeling guides you to do the right work in the world. But overall, the question is a combination of who or what influences you and why Sarah Lawrence will help you proceed with the experience you have now.

Here are some ways to respond to this question:

- Developing a voice takes years of participating in activities and reflecting on your contributions and feelings about them. So far, I have … Attending Sarah Lawrence, I will be able to take advantage of [activities, classes, location, peer network, particular professors' research, special programs, etc.] …

- Developing a voice comes partly from listening to what others have to say in response to your assertions and activities. I do this by … At [school you are applying to] I will …

- Developing a voice comes from understanding my commitment to particular projects and responsibilities. Active in [name activity],

- I have always noticed [name feelings in you connected to participating in the activity or hearing appreciation for your contributions]. At [school you are applying to], I will continue to develop my understanding of who I am and how I can make a difference in the world by [describe what you will take advantage of at the college, being very specific to your understanding of what the college offers].

- Developing a voice means reflecting on the way my activities, responses, and reactions have helped me find the activities and areas of interest right for me. [Name several of your activities and then offer a reflection on how each has helped you see who you are, your strengths, and desires for your future. Be sure to include a range of activities: intellectual, social, spiritual, athletic, artistic, people-oriented, or solo]. [Describe what you will take advantage of at the college, being very specific to your understanding of what the college offers.]

- I have developed my voice by paying attention to what has influenced me. [Name particular people, events, and activities.] [Describe what you will take advantage of at the college, being very specific to your understanding of what the college offers.]

Perfect Phrases for Organizing and Writing about Several Accomplishments and Experiences in One Essay That Show Your Superior Skills and Personality

For a little more practice in recognizing question patterns, let's consider the University of California's application essay questions, which require students to use 1,000 words to answer a combination of three questions. Each of the three essay questions includes a "rationale" explaining what the state system seeks and welcomes in its candidates.

In question 1, the rationale states that the system seeks "to enroll on each of its campuses an entering class that is academically superior and that embodies a wide range of talents, experiences, achievements, and points of view." The question is stated like this:

Describe the qualities and accomplishments you would bring to the undergraduate student body at the University of California.

This question allows you to write from the intellectual pursuits question, the leadership question, the important activities question, or the diversity question (if the slant is toward extraordinary experience and enrichment from it). Most of all, you need to show how the background you are claiming (whether that is intellectual, leadership, or awards and service accomplishments) makes you just the person the university is looking for: talented, academically superior, and with accomplishments under your belt.

The Santa Monica High School English Department Web site offers these words written by Rob Thais:

> Qualities mean character traits, talents, attitudes, and values, ways you think. Accomplishments means impressive stuff you have DONE. The prompt also mentions "experiences," so you may include significant experiences, too, but don't discuss only experiences.

This is the kind of question that allows students who have excelled and found meaning in several activities to show how the accomplishments all came together to help make them who they are today.

Imagine this essay in three parts:

- **Part 1:** I am most proud of these accomplishments: [name them showing a variety among the categories of intellectual, cultural, athletic, community service.]

- **Part 2:** In each of these experiences, I learned an important element of what it means to be [a good student, a good member of my community, a person who can make a difference, something that indicates your desire to apply what you learned from gaining awards to a lifetime of contributing].

- **Part 3:** I have already begun to apply what I have learned by [name activities and actions you have taken]. In college, I plan to [articulate how you'll use your skill and knowledge to benefit from and contribute to the college you plan to attend].

Perfect Phrases for Showing Your Potential to Contribute

The University of California system question number 2 has this rationale:

> UC welcomes the contributions each student brings to the campus learning community. This question seeks to determine an applicant's academic or creative interests and potential to contribute to the vitality of the University. The question is stated this way: Tell us about a talent, experience, contribution or personal quality you will bring to the University of California.

This question allows you to pump one academic or creative interest for all it is worth and fully describe how you have explored an area and flourished in it by receiving an award, making an impact, or being otherwise recognized. This creative or intellectual pursuit can include sports accomplishments and community impact. You might even take one of the achievements discussed in the first question and provide more detail. As Rob Thais advises, "one dramatic strategy is to tell chronologically the preparation for the achievement, and have the achievement itself be the climax of your essay. You could tell 'what you gained from it' either as you describe each preparatory step or at the end."

Your answer will benefit from addressing these four points as parts in the essay:

1. I have attained some recognition in [name of an activity], an activity that fosters [name valuable skills and/or traits].

   ■ I have attained some recognition for my chess playing, an activity that helps me think strategically and display patience. At college, I will use these skills to plan my schedule and meet deadlines as well as stick with things when they are difficult.

2. I developed my skill by [discuss the step-by-step process of becoming good at what you do].

   ■ I developed my skill in leading sing-a-longs by asking many who have done them what they like best in such an evening. After I heard their comments, which were about song choices, musical accompaniment, and sheets of music to follow, in addition to refreshments, I started a series for my neighborhood. I believe I have honed good communication and motivation skills that I can apply in class and outside of class activities.

3. As a consequence of exploring [name the activity, talent, or experience you are talking about], I am prepared to bring the following ethics, skills, and understanding to my peers and professors: [name them].

   ■ As a consequence of exploring horseback riding as a hobby, I am prepared to bring the following ethics, skills, and understanding to my peers and professors: the capacity to be disciplined in my commitment, the capacity to take responsibility for another's well being, and the capacity to follow protocol for achieving the ends I want.

4. I look forward to [name what you will do at school that will allow you to share the skills and growth you experienced].

   ■ I look forward to becoming a tutor at college because I enjoy helping others skillfully understand something I have learned and believe has value.

Perfect Phrases for Answering the Obstacles Question

The University of California's third question's rationale is this: "This question seeks to give students the opportunity to share important aspects of their schooling or their lives— such as their personal circumstances, family experiences and opportunities that were or were not available at their school or college that may not have been sufficiently addressed elsewhere in the application." The question is stated this way: "Is there anything you would like us to know about you or your academic record that you have not had the opportunity to describe elsewhere in this application?"

The university wants to know, Ron Thais writes, if you've had tougher obstacles to overcome than the average student, so that what "you've accomplished has been in spite of these obstacles, and is therefore more impressive. This prompt is especially appropriate for ethnic/racial minorities; immigrants; people with physical, emotional, or learning handicaps; and people with especially difficult financial or family problems."

If you don't fall into one of those categories, you might still have a wonderful story to tell about yourself—similar to the Sarah Lawrence essay about whether you feel you have developed a voice and how college will help you do this.

- When I heard [name of person] say, "[a quote]," I felt sure that I hadn't had the high school opportunities required for [name accomplishment or work you wanted to prepare for]. I know I have missed out on learning [name areas] because of [name the cause—poor school program, poverty, illness, family difficulties, location]. However, I have begun to address this loss in the following ways: [list a combination of things that show you are reading in the area, seeking information and answers, and finding a mentor to help you]. Now, I believe that … [make a statement that you can then support about how you will do well in college and use resources available to you].

Or:

- So far in my life, I have encountered many obstacles: [list them]. I've tried to be creative in how I have dealt with each one: [show how you handled them]. The outcome for me was [name your successes and failures and the strengths you developed]. By my experiences, I believe I am better prepared to deal with the challenges college presents [mention some challenges and how you're prepared to take them on as a student].

Part Three

Tricks of the Trade for Polished Essays

Chapter 11
On Writing Strong Beginnings, Middles, and Endings

On Openings

To write a compelling college application essay, you need to draw readers into your experience without using too many words to set the scene. You have to get to the heart of the matter quickly and, at the same time, make the reader want to read on. Visualizing a particular moment from a situation that disappointed or thrilled you, you'll see that you can start an essay about a disappointment, an obstacle, an intellectual or creative passion, or a lucky break with a short scene.

Following are three examples to help you do this with your opening paragraph or two.

Opening Essays with Scenes

Here is an opening scene for an answer to the question about how a student faced disappointment and learned from a mistake:

I stared at the "C" in red ink above my name. I had wanted to impress Mr. Burns, who was head of the AP English courses I wanted to take the following year. My story involved a boy who suffered when his father was on trial for a white-collar crime. Reading Mr. Burns's comments, I saw he was questioning the idea that my character would leave his family when his mother and siblings most needed him. I thought the leaving was a good plot idea, but now I realized I had to figure out why this action didn't seem likely to my teacher.

I stared at the red mark during my next class, which was psychology. Mrs. Applebaum was presenting information on post-traumatic stress disorder. She described some of symptoms as "irrational and maladaptive behaviors." A light bulb went on! Perhaps my character had seen his father led away in handcuffs and was suffering from post-traumatic stress disorder. Perhaps when he saw his family, he was afraid that more of them would be led away, and he didn't want to see that so he ran away. How could I insert this information in my story without turning fiction into a psychology paper?

Here is an opening scene for an essay about an activity a student is passionate about:

My father showed us a home video shot when I was in kindergarten, and I saw my young self at my older brother's electronic keyboard. I seemed happy playing "Row, Row, Row Your Boat" for an audience of Teddy bears. I realized I've always smiled when I am playing a tune or classical piece for others. After many years of study, today I am pianist in the Rhode Island State High School Orchestra. Not only have I performed on the eastern seaboard, but I have traveled to Europe and the Mediterranean with the orchestra and heard many fine orchestras and played with their musicians.

Here is an opening scene for an essay about someone who has influenced you:

On Writing Strong Beginnings, Middles, and Endings

I keep a photograph in my desk drawer of me at age three, wearing a flowery dress and tiny gold earrings. I am sitting on my grandparents' couch holding my infant cousin Deena. I look at the camera with a serious expression because I am aware of my responsibility to be careful with this tiny baby. Deena's eyes are open, and she is staring at me. I did not know that our friendship would change my life.

Here is an opening scene for an essay about an intellectual passion:

Walking with my mother on a family vacation to Michigan, I came across the house my grandparents had lived in and my great grandparents before them. I thought about my ancestors who had come to the United States from Holland, as my mother described bleached *brukes* hung out to dry on a clothesline and toothbrushes used to clean the cracks between bathroom tiles with bleach. I thought of the fact that I don't have to hang laundry out to dry or put as much elbow grease into getting rid of dirt. I felt fortunate, but I also thought about the need we have now to become environmentally aware about the household chemicals we use that contaminate our water and soil. Wondering about what harmless ingredients might work as cleaners, I decided to research products in the hopes of figuring out how to least harm the environment while not having to expend the energy my grandparents did.

Perfect Phrases for Visualizing Moments and Situations

As you remember, these phrases come from the opening exercises about using words that force writers to immerse themselves in the situations they're writing about. Don't forget to make lists of what you tasted, smelled, heard, saw, and felt in the scene you're describing so you can add these images and help the reader get into your essay:

- **I tasted . . .**
  - I tasted the unfamiliar dish made with wild boar.
  - I tasted the spinach and mashed potatoes my grandmother made and didn't mind eating the green vegetable.

- **I smelled . . .**
  - I smelled the paper mill and knew I was nearly home.
  - My new baby sister smelled like peaches.

- **I heard . . .**
  - I heard sleigh bells and the clop of the horses' hooves.
  - I heard the ferries' foghorns all day, which ignited a deep longing in me to see farther than my own small world.

- **I saw . . .**
  - I saw my mother's hat in the crowd.
  - I saw two raccoons climbing the tree where we'd hung our backpacks.

- **I felt . . .**
  - I felt the warm sand on my feet.
  - I felt the rain soak through my shoes.

If you're writing about details you learned second hand that made an impression on you, change the grammar to help yourself gather images by changing the "I" to "Someone told me . . ."

Opening Essays with Direct Speech or a Quote

Here is an opening for an essay about overcoming an obstacle or about an experience or person who influenced you. It might also be for an essay about learning leadership skills:

- "What do you want to get from our time together?" the physical trainer asked. "I'm not exactly sure. I just thought that it might help me feel stronger by the time I report to duty as a camp counselor this summer," I replied, feeling foolish. I was embarrassed explaining that getting a job as a counselor for 10-year-olds made me fear I wouldn't be a strong enough swimmer and hiker, let alone rower, for them to respect me.

Here is an opening for an essay about an ethical dilemma:

- "What do you think about me retiring?" my father asked me as my feet sank into the warm Big Sur sand. I didn't mean it when I told him that I thought it took strength and conviction to step down as CEO of the company he had built, a company I had spent my childhood hearing about and my high school years working for, a company my mother felt brought us financial stability. I didn't know how to say that I didn't think the family was ready for him to give up a job he'd been passionate about for a decade.

Here is an opening for an essay on a volunteer experience:

- "Hello," I said with an outstretched hand and a smile. "I'm David." Robert, who is as well built as a professional baseball player, is mentally challenged. He stared at his feet and wouldn't shake my hand. Although he had received services from our local organization for the developmentally disabled since birth, he was still a shy person. At this point, even though I wasn't sure I would ever feel comfortable in my new volunteer position, I was motivated to help people like Robert because I'd read a news story that disturbed me—some boys from my school had threatened and chased a person like Robert. I wanted to do what I could to create better understanding among my high school peers.

Here is an opening for an essay about family experiences:

- "Everything is going to be all right," my father had assured me. He must have been wondering what would become of us if something happened to him. I was the only one of his three children who lived at home and knew of his health problems. My sister was away in dental school facing her exams. My brother was overseas reporting on events in Turkey, filing stories that would earn him a promotion. My mother and I listened as my father told the nurse about his pounding headache and vomiting. I realized that I had never seen my father sick in bed with even the flu. He was a strong man who always took care of us.

Here is an opening for a diversity essay:

■ Hello. Hola. I came to this country from Mexico City when I was eight years old. I didn't speak English, but I entered second grade, and within six months, I was fluent. I owe this to my classmates and to the successful ESL program in my town.

Here's an opening for a why-this-school essay:

■ "The best public school is the University of Connecticut; it has a phenomenal business school and school of pharmacy. However, its engineering programs really separate the school from others." I read this on Yahoo Answers while looking for information on public East Coast colleges and universities my family could afford. Since I have hopes of starting my own engineering company some day, this information was inspiring. I conducted more research and soon became convinced that UConn was my first choice of school.

Perfect Phrases for Helping You Remember Dialogue or Quotes That Could Open an Essay

Significant sentences people have said to me at particular moments include:

- "'Go West, young man!' That's what I read as a youngster, and doing so has made all the difference," my grandfather said as I was debating going to college in my home state of California or trying out the East Coast. His words reminded me of why I want to stay where I've grown up.

- "If you want a friend, be a friend," my mother always said when I complained about being lonely my freshman year in a new high school.

When I think about influential people in my life, I remember them saying:

- "Fortunately, the ranks of politicians and corporate executives include mature individuals committed to maintaining the highest ethical standards, but they often find themselves at a disadvantage in a system that forces them to continuously compete for their positions against those unburdened by conscience or compassion" are the words of author and activist David Korten in an interview he did with *Sun Magazine*. They sum up why I want to study political science and become a policy maker.

- "As a poet, you must learn to write in more than one genre, because there will be times the poems won't come," my first poetry teacher, David Wagoner, told me. Right then I resolved to study playwriting as well as poetry writing.

A quote that stays with me about the school I want to attend is:

- In the Fall 2007 *On Wisconsin* alumni magazine, Michael Penn writes, "UW–Madison's 56-percent acceptance rate is on par with its peer flagship institutions, such as Michigan (47 percent) and Illinois (65 percent)." I am proud to live in a state that supports qualified students in achieving a fine higher education.
- The Colorado College Web site describes an arts event, "As the sun began to set behind Pikes Peak, the first act of an experimental student production got under way." Theater is my passion, and Colorado College's cutting edge performances attract me.

Questions people have asked me that were important for me to answer:

- "What is it exactly that you find so interesting about collecting butterflies?" my aunt has asked me on her yearly visit ever since I was six. My answers have grown more elaborate over the years.
- "If you knew whatever cause you advocated would attract money and followers like Madonna's and Angelina Jolie's, what cause would you choose to speak out for?" my social studies teacher asked. I knew immediately. I want to work on behalf of cleaning up our planet's water supply.

Opening Essays with Assertions or Facts

Here is an opening for an essay that discusses intellectual interests:

- As a student at one of Illinois' specialized high schools, I have developed a strong interest in psychology and biology; in addition, I delved into creative writing while attending Barnard College's summer writing program for high school students. I would like to combine my interests in these fields and begin studies to become a poetry therapist and mental health writer.

Here is an opening for an essay about social concerns:

- Reading about the last one hundred years of world history, I count incredible advancements in civil rights, psychology, technology, and physics, among other fields, but I also acknowledge loss. A world without chemical weapons or atomic bombs is impossible now, when only one hundred years ago, not even military aircraft existed.

Here is an opening for an essay about an important life experience:

- I was seven years old when my father was transferred and my family moved to Micronesia. Needless to say, I was terrified and unsure of what to expect. I was quiet at school, taking in the cultural differences and not sure of how to act. One day, I was invited to my French classmate Jacques' house. I didn't think it would be easy, but wanting so much to have a friend, I went. At dinner, I listened to the family speaking in French and didn't understand a word. When someone laughed, I wondered what they found funny. Sometimes someone would ask me a question in English and then would go back to the French conversation. I didn't think the evening was going to get any better, but after dinner, Jacques' brothers asked me if I wanted to play PlayStation with them. I knew then that despite differences in their language and the food they ate, these boys were like me.

Perfect Phrases for Writing Assertions That Open an Essay

- **I have always enjoyed [name of subjects or activities], and this enjoyment has led to [name of study or career goal].**
  - I have always enjoyed music class, and this enjoyment has led to my learning what it takes to become a music therapist.
  - I have enjoyed biology and zoology classes in high school and have researched docent opportunities at the college's zoo and botanical gardens hoping I could do volunteer work there.

- **When I was [specific age], I [name of an event: moved, was hospitalized, learned about something in particular, won an award].**
  - When I was 14, my parents moved back to China, and I stayed in the United States to finish high school and get into a good college.
  - When I was 10, I was out of school for a year while I wore a cast to correct a spine curvature.

- **When I was asked to [name of an activity you participated in], I was sure that I would [describe what you thought would happen, good or bad].**
  - When I was asked to coordinate a student poetry reading series at our town's community center, I was sure that I would have trouble finding students courageous enough to read in front of an audience.
  - When I was asked to coordinate a collection of money to

donate a gift to the school, I didn't think it was going to be difficult. That was before I realized how hard it is to ask for money without offering something immediate in return.

- **I will always [name an activity you will do or something you will remember].**
  - I will always remember the night I hatched the idea of collecting money for our class gift by starting a pyramid scheme involving amassing walnuts, which would later be used as currency to have your name inscribed on the gift as the one who raised the most funds.
  - I will always remember the second-grade girls in the inner city of Los Angeles to whom I taught ballet two days a week for a whole school year.

On Middles

Strong middles are filled with images and details just as successful openings are, but they also involve commentary, analysis, support for assertions, and transitional clauses to move the reader from the evocation of a situation to a portrait of its impact and importance. After an opening that hooks readers with specifics to draw them closer to the writer's life, middles may start with the thesis statement you've written for your material and then go on to support it.

Following is the middle of the essay that began with the opening about an applicant's family being relocated to Micronesia. His opening centers on a breakthrough experience while visiting his friend Jacques. It continues with a middle that widens the lens and shows more about what he learned over the year with his new schoolmates. A statement about this diversity experience is supported with a list of details (the importance of Asian elders, European football, stadium food, holidays, for instance) and with commentary (I enjoy living these values).

Words and phrases like "ultimately," "now that," "meanwhile," and "after my experiences" supply transitions between sentences that allow the writer's argument to build.

> Ultimately, I shared my CDs and music magazines with all the students I met at my international school in Micronesia. In turn, they increased my understanding of cultural diversity. I learned about the importance of elders in Asian communities and how in Italy dinner is important for spending time with family and friends. My European friends taught me to play soccer, which is European football, and I explained why stadium food in the United States is delicious to me. We shared our different national holidays and enjoyed the same music

and electronics. We spoke different languages, but we learned we had similar fears and dreams.

Now that I am home in the United States, I look forward to studying in a diverse student body, one that includes international students from many different economic backgrounds. Meanwhile, I pay attention to pop culture slogans like, "Be true to yourself" and "Commit random acts of kindness." After my experiences in Micronesia and my understanding of how good it feels to connect with others rather than be isolated, I enjoy living these values.

Perfect Phrases for Making Transitions

■ **Ultimately**
- Ultimately, I motivated 120 students to collect a total of $4,000.
- Ultimately, I worked with a mentor at our city's butterfly garden.

■ **Moreover**
- Moreover, I learned that working alongside others helps everyone keep on task.
- Moreover, I have decided that dance will be my major.

■ **In addition**
- In addition, my town's city government kicked in matching funds of $4,000.
- In addition, I started teaching a Saturday butterfly class for fifth graders.

■ **As it turned out**
- As it turned out, I recognized that I had the capacity to become a skilled teacher.
- As it turned out, I realized that raising money is a difficult but doable job.

■ **After**
- After I sketched out my pyramid scheme on paper, I advertised for "salespeople."
- After three months of working with the girls, I could see the grace they'd developed through ballet.

■ **Meanwhile**
- Meanwhile, my friends were busy discussing my new passion and thinking that I couldn't be for real.

- Meanwhile, although I told my parents not to worry about me staying alone, I was fighting my own demons about my ability to take on such a big responsibility.

- **Now that**
  - Now that the class gift has been installed, I walk past it with pride.
  - Now that the girls have put on a performance for the school and one for their parents, their self-esteem has increased greatly.

- **However**
  - However, as well as I planned, things did not go smoothly.
  - However, even with the extra hours and manpower, the task was too large to accomplish by our deadline.

- **Although**
  - Although everyone pitched in at the end and helped, one important task was left undone.
  - Although my parents did in the end let me stay on my own, my adjustment to the situation wasn't as smooth as I would have liked.

- **Taking everything into consideration**
  - Taking everything into consideration, I would say that the project was a success because it taught me to stick up for what I believe in.
  - Taking everything into consideration, although I could have performed better grade-wise my junior year, I believe I learned as much as if I'd gotten straight A's.

- **Because**
  - Because I failed to gain the GPA required to belong, I had to find another activity that would serve my interests.
  - Because my grades improved, I found myself less stressed and better able to communicate with my class-mates.

- **Whether**
  - Whether we always agreed or not, we remained commit-ted to figuring out a solution.
  - Whether the girls showed up with ballet shoes or with-out, we were able to run through the routine.

- **Interestingly**
  - Interestingly, no one objected to our proposal.
  - Interestingly, after we'd raised some funds, it was easier to raise more.

- **On the other hand**
  - On the other hand, ballet is extremely relevant to today's inner-city children as it allows them the opportunity to connect to cultures around the world.
  - On the other hand, unlike my siblings, I have always wanted to study farther from home.

- **Even though**
  - Even though I didn't get accepted to the summer pro-gram, I got to study in an independent online course.
  - Even though I put in weeks of study time and still scored lower than expected, I count my effort as successful because I learned important study skills I can apply out-side of test situations.

Following is the middle to the essay that opened with the dialogue between the writer and the personal trainer with whom he wanted to work. It makes its transition from opening to middle with one of the phrases in the list above: "As it turned out." After that transition phrase, the first sentence continues as statement of purpose concerning the action the speaker has taken and the rest of the paragraph shows how he achieved his goal. It ends on the surprise achievement, which is also a realization about what he might have feared most, that the campers would not be safe under his wing:

As it turned out, the trainer affirmed my idea that I would be a more effective counselor if I were not worried about keeping up with the kids and being able to provide a strong role model for them. The next week, I came to the health club my parents had joined, and I began working with the personal trainer to develop the muscles in my arms, legs, and chest. I also began working on endurance and proper breathing. I committed to working out three times a week, once with her and twice on my own.

I had to tuck in my workout time around my studies, homework, and other extracurriculars, such as chess club and orchestra. By using weekends, as well as an early morning before school, I was able to fit in all three sessions every week. As soon as the weather was warm enough, I rented a rowboat and timed myself across the lake where my grandparents live, pleased with how I rowed the length of it and back in 30 minutes. I went to the REI store in Seattle and climbed the synthetic mountain it uses for mountain climbing classes, reaching the top quickly and without feeling stressed. I went to a public indoor pool and swam five miles in an hour.

When summer arrived, I reported to camp feeling confident that I could earn the respect of my campers, provide a good role model, and furthermore, help keep them safe, as I was now quite strong.

After "As it turned out," the transition phrase that gets the reader from the opening to the middle of the essay, the essay is carried forward by phrases that show time passing: "The next week," "As soon as the weather was warm enough," and "When summer arrived."

Perfect Phrases for Carrying Essays Forward

- **As it turned out**
  - As it turned out, we would spend the next 40 days working on the project we thought would take one week.
  - As it turned out, my mother was grateful for my lateness because it gave her more time to hide the guests before my entrance and their yelling, "Surprise!"
  - As it turned out, none of the material was recyclable and we had to redesign our project.

- **When**
  - When people are full of dissension, it is important to remember how to point out where they do agree.
  - When I could overcome my disappointment and listen carefully, I realized the coach was giving me good advice.

- **Soon**
  - Soon all of us were canvassing our neighbors for information on how they determined whether they would recycle.
  - Soon I could barely see because tears blurred my vision.

- **In the next weeks**
  - In the next weeks, squads of kids picked up litter from every street in our town.
  - In the next weeks, I gladly performed community service rather than report to after-school detention.

- **I realized**
  - I realized that experience counts and learning from

those who have come before is essential for success.

– I realized that believing in possibilities is half the battle, and learning how to design and manage projects is the other half.

- **I started to believe**
  – I started to believe in myself as a future leader.
  – I started to believe that, for our human world to survive, we are going to have to learn to honor our interconnections and refuse to believe that dominating one another works.

Following is another middle. This one is to the essay about the candidate's feelings of loss in a world that can't go back to a time when mass destruction was not as possible:

Going to school amidst talk of military surges in Iraq, a reinstated draft, and reports that the most dangerous terrorists may be homegrown, I am sometimes envious of my grandparents who fought in World War II and lived through the depression. The country muddled through the depression and won the war, which ushered in a time of technological and medical advancement that raised standards of living and educational advancement. People could feasibly commute to better jobs, be treated for the prevention of illnesses like polio that would previously have had them bedridden or maimed, and good housing was built quickly in the post-war period, allowing families to spread out and enjoy freedom from cultural restraints. America was fast becoming a melting pot where men and women could rise to the middle or upper classes and ensure a great future for their children.

Today, as I enter college, I see mugs for sale at the gift store of my local science center that proclaim, "Watch the coastlines disappear!" Rents and home prices seem to far outstrip what a typical college graduate can afford, and the prospect of sharing homes with family members or other young adults seems likely. The government is talking about withdrawal from Iraq taking years. Covert surveillance to protect our nation from terrorist attacks hinders personal freedom of speech and makes for an atmosphere of fear.

Still, instead of being depressed, I find myself stirred by the values instilled in me by my parents: optimism, stick-to-it-ive-ness, and enthusiasm. I am inspired by activities that bring out the best in us, such as space exploration, digital and electronic technology, and medical research that is unlocking secrets of the brain.

Additional Perfect Phrases for Carrying Your Essay Forward

■ **Going to [a place or an event], I [an action you took or a thought you had] ...**

- Going to Vietnam for a vacation with my parents, I sat on the beautiful beaches and tried to imagine a country torn by war, as it was during my parents' high school years.

- Going to the Tanglewood outdoor summer concert, I realized I wanted to intern at the theater and learn about creating events that brought people together.

■ **We (I) are (am) sometimes ...**

- I am sometimes wary of my future because I know there will be technological advances that will change life as I know it.

- We are all sometimes slow to get a point. I realize when I am tutoring that although I know the subject I am helping a student with, there are many subjects I would have a hard time understanding.

■ **We (I) could ...**

- We could definitely use more medical practitioners trained in advocating for the aging, because this population sees many specialists, takes many medications, and often has no one remembering to follow through with a physician's advice and request to check up on them.

- We could certainly have given up, but instead, we redoubled our efforts because the goal was important to us.

- **Today ...**
  - Today we are 1,000 strong in our state and march each year to remind people about the value of cleaning litter from the streets.
  - Today, I am studying ballet with an increased passion because I believe that along with performing, I will always be teaching young children the pleasures of this art.

- **Next year ...**
  - Next year at college, I will miss my family and have already figured out how I will stay in close contact using an online blog called LiveJournal.
  - Next year, after my first semester is finished, I believe I will look back at my high school preparation and thank my teachers who made me work hard.

- **Still ...**
  - Still, I continue to be an optimist and believe individuals make a difference.
  - Still, I will work hard to create another endeavor in which I can use the lessons I learned from my recent failure.

On Endings

A successful ending has to draw the material to a valid conclusion and loop back to the opening in a way that makes readers realize they have been on a journey, and though back where they started, they are transformed in some way. The speaker began in a specific place, physically and emotionally, took readers through a process, and brought them safely back to solid ground. A successful ending allows readers to exit the essay satisfied, not feeling left out of important information, thoughts, or conclusions.

Here is more of the middle and then the ending to the essay about feeling the loss in a world capable of mass destruction:

> Because of my interest in science, I want to contribute to society through engineering, applied to medicine or military surveillance equipment. As an undergraduate, I will gain a thorough foundation in physics and chemistry, as I believe the future of engineering is biology-based and our digital equipment will run on energy from plankton. Our bodies will benefit from implants made of biological material. Because of this, at college, I will participate in the debate team, specializing on bioethical issues. I will also look for internships where I can shadow physicians doing medical research and professors who are developing cutting edge bio-electronic equipment. I hope to be accepted for a work-study job as a research assistant.

> Though I can't do much directly about the nuclear shadow we leave under and the ways in which the world includes many warring factions, I can contribute to the quality of lives in the hopes that by maintaining the health of people and our planet, I'll help advance the human capacity for preserving life.

And here is an ending to the essay about the student who increased his physical strength so he could feel like a good counselor:

> Once camp started and I met my six bunk charges, I relaxed. Each little guy weighed about 70 pounds to my 135. They immediately looked up to me, finding my deep voice and biceps worthy of respect. They enjoyed my teaching them the details of holding an oar and placing themselves properly in a rowboat. I also taught them how to efficiently scoop rain water out of the boat's bottom before we took off on the lake. We played tennis and basketball and went to a quarry to learn how to rappel. My boys voted me the best swimming instructor because I knew how to help them learn to lengthen their endurance and increase their speed. I told them of the mornings I trudged out before dawn while every else was still asleep and entered the bright, busy world of the gym to do my workout. By not being afraid or embarrassed to address what I had considered my weakness, I turned my insecurity into something that helped others bond and grow strong.

There are no exact perfect phrases for endings—every ending is a product of a beginning. When you feel your essay has satisfied its promise to its readers and has in some way looped full circle back to the opening without repeating it, you have reached your ending. After you've studied the sample endings in this section, compare them to the openings of the same essays earlier in this chapter. You will get a feel for the individual ways endings refer back to openings.

Questions for Evaluating Your Ending

Here are some ways you can evaluate whether your essay has looped to the beginning and left the reader satisfied.

On Writing Strong Beginnings, Middles, and Endings

■ What words and images in my closing make me remember the opening of my essay?

■ If they are different from the words I used in my opening, how do they relate to that opening?

■ If they are the same, what keeps them from being merely repetitious?

■ Have I included enough facts and details to make the reader believe in my conclusion and the way it relates to my opening?

■ If I have made a statement that brings the most salient point in my essay forward, have I done so without starting on a new topic that my essay does not support?

Chapter 12
Additional Editing and Formatting Tips

Editing and Polishing Your Essay

After you've developed your essay from topic and thesis statement to smooth, strong openings, middles, and endings, you must take the time to look at your work with an editor's eye. You should also have trusted readers do this with you so you can test out how others follow your words. They will tell you if something nongrammatical has thrown them and if they find spelling errors or patches that lack clarity. Since you want to avoid wordiness, vagueness, awkwardness, and clichés, these readers should tell you about any places they come across these problems and are jolted out of the experience they're reading.

Common Grammar Errors to Watch For

Dangling modifiers: They creep into essays when the writer is offering complicated ideas in a compressed form. "Turning six, my father decided it was time to teach me to hunt," is a sentence with a dangling modifier: The child is turning six, not the father. It would be correct to write, "When I was turning six, my father decided it was time for me to learn to hunt," or, "Turning six, I learned to hunt as my father decided it was time." When you have a phrase that starts with an "ing" word, make sure that this phrase is not modifying the wrong noun or pronoun.

Restrictive and nonrestrictive phrases—which to set off with commas: When a noun or pronoun is modified by a phrase that is necessary to knowing who the person, event, or object is, that phrase is *not* set off with commas: The man who was wearing the blue hat, the dog with the loud bark, the corner where the traffic stops, for instance, all have what we call restrictive phrases modifying them—these are necessary for knowing which man, which dog, and which corner the writer means, so no commas are used. However, if I said, "My Uncle Harry, who was wearing a blue hat, wanted to take me to dinner," I would need commas to set off the phrase "who was wearing a blue hat" because in this case, it is a nonrestrictive phrase. Uncle Harry is a proper noun and is therefore always Uncle Harry, whether or not he is wearing the blue hat. Who he is is not restricted by the further information.

More examples: In the sentence beginning, "My neighbor's dog Trudy, who had a loud bark," the descriptive phrase is nonrestrictive and *is* set off with commas. In the modifying phrase in "the corner of Westin and 4th Avenue, where the traffic stops," the nonrestrictive phrase "where the traffic stops" is set off with commas.

Run-on sentences: If you have more than one independent clause (a sentence with a subject and verb that offers a complete thought), it can't be connected to another independent clause with a comma. It requires a semicolon to do that. Most often, you would use a period and begin the second independent clause as a separate sentence. You can also use a conjunction to link the sentences, and you put a comma before the conjunction (and, but, or, nor).

Interesting: The words *however* and *therefore* are not conjunctions and they *do* require commas to set them apart from the rest of the independent clause they belong to:

- Someone ran into the room and ordered students to evacuate the building because of a funny smell. However, I had gone home early that day.
- Someone ran into the room and ordered students to evacuate the building because of a funny smell; however, I had gone home early that day.
- I want to study engineering, and I want to study dance. Therefore, I believe NYU is the school for me.
- I want to study engineering and dance, and, therefore, I believe NYU is the school for me.
- I want to study engineering and dance; therefore, I believe NYU is the school for me.

Plural pronouns: It used to be that when you said something like, "A reader must know what he is getting into," you had to choose between he or she because *reader* is singular. There are some who believe that it's OK to write, "A reader must know what they are getting into." This seems to promote gender equality, but it sounds awkward and is not grammatically correct. In this sitaution, writers should see if they can change the pronoun's referent to plural and maintain the meaning, "Readers must know what they are getting into" sounds much smoother.

Homonyms: There are many words in English that sound alike but have different spellings. Here and hear; know and no; two, too, and to; bear and bare; their, they're, and there; weather and whether; witch and which are among those that are commonly mixed up. When you check for spelling using a computer spell checker, the spell checker will not usually mark a misused homonym as misspelled. Since all of us sometimes type one with the wrong meaning without thinking, let someone you believe is a good speller and knows English grammar well read over your work for incorrectly used homonyms. You might also refresh your memory and theirs about those words we commonly mix up by studying a list of homonyms. You can find such lists online at sites like **www.cooper.com/alan/homonym_list.html** and **www.earlham.edu/~peters/writing/homofone.htm**.

Contractions are two words made into one using an apostrophe. You'll notice that in a contraction the apostrophe appears where a letter is omitted. This is always the case with contractions: do not becomes don't, and cannot becomes can't, for instance.

Note: Many homonyms involve contractions (aisle and I'll; your and you're; there, they're, and their; we're, where, and wear, for instance). Moreover, if you're contracting a word with a verb, the apostrophe is necessary (it's, who's, there'll, they're, you're, I'll, for example), but if you're showing possession using a pronoun, no apostrophe is needed (its, hers, his, theirs, yours).

The possessive: To show possession you add an apostrophe-*s* to a noun or pronoun: the children's room, the boy's father, the truck's wheel, the people's park. Adding an *s* to make something plural (writers, books, taxis, for instance) *never* requires an apostrophe. If a word is already plural and you want to show possession, add apostrophe-*s* after the last letter, except in the case where the last letter is an *s*. If there is already an *s*, you may just add the apostrophe to avoid the *z* sound another *s* would cause: in books', writers', and taxis', for instance.

Remember: It's means it is. It is not the same as *its*, which means belonging to it. Plural nouns are made plural with the addition of an *s* or an *ies*, not an apostrophe-*s*. Watch that you haven't mistakenly put apostrophes into words when they don't need to be there.

Word choice: English is full of precise words and the more intangible the meaning and the less we read such abstract words in proper contexts, the more we mix up the words when we use them. Ben Yagoda, an English professor who wrote *When You Catch an Adjective, Kill It: The Parts of Speech, for Better and/or Worse*, points out that "aspired" does not mean the same as "expected," "accredited" does not mean the same as "attributed," "invade" does not mean "dominate," "blame" is not the same as "accuse," "a vast proportion" does not mean "a majority," "rejuvenated" does not mean "refurbished" or "energized."

Here are student examples he includes in his article about student mistakes (reprinted at **www.uky.edu/~rst/Yagoda%20on %20Writing.pdf**.

- Of the many things the students aspired [expected] to see, a terrorist attack was not one of them.
- The drop in candidates can be accredited [attributed] to . . .
- Stories about the hurricane invade [dominate] the entire first section of the newspaper.
- No one can blame [accuse] John Henrickson of being an apathetic college student.

■ The vast proportion [majority] of students is enrolled in the College of Arts and Science.

Yagoda diagnoses the problem of improper word choice this way, "Skilled writers profit from a continuously looping, subliminal soundtrack of all the sentences they've ever read. The students who do not have such a soundtrack fall back on the archive of conversations that are in their heads. The spoken language follows a different protocol . . . . "

What this means to me is: Of course, you should look up words that you're using that you don't normally use or that you suspect you might not have used correctly. Then, have someone who loves reading and has done a lot of it review your essay and tell you if you've used your selection of abstract words well. This means those words that stand for a concept rather than a specific. Conversely, where you have used too many words to explain a concept, this kind of reader might be able to help you out with a word to replace a phrase. Write the word down. Look it up in a dictionary. Add it to the list of words you can use in your college writing. *Penultimate* is a word I learned that allows me to shorten sentences. Now I never have to say "next to the last" anymore!

Although you shouldn't start using "big" words just because you're writing an essay for your college application, neither should you forget that they can help you sound articulate and save you from many word tangles.

Perfect Words for Shortening Phrases

■ Penultimate (rather than "next to the last")
■ To (rather than "in order to")
■ Many (rather than "a lot")

- Seven people completed the whole run (rather than, "The run was completed by seven people").
- My uncle gave me a job (rather than, "I was given a job by my uncle").
- We decided to leave the fund-raising up to the adults (rather than, "We decided that a good choice would be to leave the fund-raising up to the adults").
- I decided (rather than "I made the decision to").
- I concluded (rather than, "I came to the conclusion that").
- When I viewed the movie (rather than, "When I was able to view the movie").
- Arnie, an accomplished baseball player with lots of experience coaching, helped me prepare for the tryouts (instead of, "Arnie is an accomplished baseball player and has lots of experience coaching. He helped me prepare for the try-outs").
- My experience as a citizen reporter for an online news site will help me learn from conflict situations at college (rather than, "My very unique experience as a citizen reporter for an online news site will help me learn from conflict situations at college"). Delete the word *very* since if something is unique, it is already one of a kind. How much more one-of-a-kind can it be? I don't believe the word *unique* is needed either—details show rather than tell.
- We came out of the ocean shivering from the 40-degree water we'd just subjected ourselves to. (Rather than, "We came out of the ocean shivering from 40-degree water we'd just subjected ourselves to. We were very cold.") It's already obvious from the details that you were cold.

Additional Editing and Formatting Tips

- Using his small-motor dexterity, my dentist father made model planes with me (rather than, "My father is a dentist, and he used his small motor dexterity to make model planes with me.").
- When Kelly and I came around the corner, our mouths opened in surprise (rather than, "When Kelly and I came around the corner, our mouths opened. We were so surprised! We could hardly talk or even laugh. It was awesome.").

Obviously, not fatiguing the reader and meeting word length limits are connected—you want to use the "real estate" apportioned to you for your personal essay to keep the reader awake and touring the property. You want to make sure you've put the most important information in the space available so the visit is noteworthy. You don't want to have to leave something out because unimportant phrases, no matter how much they sound like you when you're talking, have cluttered up the lot.

According to Linda Abraham of **Accepted.com**, when an essay is 20 to 30 percent over the essay guideline or word limit, "It needs editing, not major surgery. I don't really want to cut content, but I must cut verbiage. I look for clues, signs of lazy writing. These quirky writing tics tell me I can edit without taking away from the story line or changing the writer's voice."

After you've gotten rid of the "tics," you can look at the essay again asking yourself, "Do my readers really need to know this? In what way is it important?" You'll probably find that some of the conjunctions you used, thinking you had to connect things, aren't necessary. The reader is already making the connection: "I went into the kitchen and when I heard a loud noise in the living room, I quickly walked toward the kitchen door and into the hallway that leads to the living room." This can be shortened: "When I heard a loud noise coming from the living room, I ran to see what had happened."

Finally, before you submit your essay, once again spell and grammar check, and if you are in doubt as to whether the software is correct in what it's suggesting, consult your English teacher or anyone who writes a lot for their work—tech writers, copyeditors, and freelance writers are good bets.

Formatting and Uploading Your Essay

Now it's time to be sure you get the application and essay shipped off to the colleges you're applying to. First of all, stop running the editing program you're using. If it's "track changes" in Microsoft Word, accept all changes and unclick the "track changes" choice. Then copy and paste your finalized document into a fresh document on your computer. This will guarantee that all the edits and comments made and inserted don't show up on the version you submit. Check your margins, line spacing, font choice, and font size. Make sure they conform to what the schools' guidelines require.

A visit to **www.commonapp.org/CommonApp/Instructions.aspx** will inform you about making online and mailed application submissions, which include the Common Application and school-specific supplemental essays.

Look at the way you've done paragraphing—if you haven't indented the beginning of paragraphs (used block form), you must make an extra space between paragraphs. If you've indented the first line of each paragraph, don't put an extra space between the paragraphs. Indenting paragraphs saves room when there is a page limit length.

Be sure to polish edit the rest of the words and data in your application—your essay and all your application materials should look as if they received your full attention.

And one last word of advice: If you're submitting online, don't wait until the last day to submit (and certainly not until the last few hours of that day!). The process of uploading takes time, and if hundreds are submitting at the same time as you are, you're going to have trouble. Organize yourself to get your application finished and submitted a few days prior to the absolute deadline. Then on deadline day, enjoy yourself with a movie, favorite book, or TV show! Or, if you've convinced your friends to be as diligent as you have been, and they, too, are finished applying, you might all celebrate together!

Perfect Phrases for Congratulating Yourself and Celebrating

- Hooray, I did it!
- I'm done, done, done!
- I think I actually like writing!
- I know I'll be able to face English composition!
- Writing has taught me a lot about thinking deeply and organizing my thoughts.
- I sound good on paper and believe in myself.
- Thank you, essay writing, for making me a stronger college candidate!

PERFECT PHRASES

for...

MANAGERS

Perfect Phrases for
Managers and Supervisors

Perfect Phrases for Setting
Performance Goals

Perfect Phrases for
Performance Reviews

Perfect Phrases for
Motivating and Rewarding
Employees

Perfect Phrases for
Documenting Employee
Performance Problems

Perfect Phrases for Business
Proposals and Business Plans

Perfect Phrases for
Customer Service

Perfect Phrases for
Executive Presentations

Perfect Phrases for Business
Letters

Perfect Phrases for the
Sales Call

Perfect Phrases for Perfect
Hiring

Perfect Phrases for Building
Strong Teams

Perfect Phrases for Dealing
with Difficult People

YOUR CAREER

Perfect Phrases for the
Perfect Interview

Perfect Phrases for
Resumes

Perfect Phrases for Negotiating
Salary & Job Offers

Perfect Phrases for Cover
Letters